QUEEN
JULIANA

WILLIAM HOFFMAN

QUEEN JULIANA

The Story of
the Richest Woman
in the World

Harcourt Brace Jovanovich
New York and London

Requests for permission to make copies of
any part of the work should be mailed to:
Permissions, Harcourt Brace Jovanovich, Inc.
757 Third Avenue, New York, N.Y. 10017

Printed in the United States of America

LIBRARY OF CONGRESS CATALOGING IN PUBLICATION DATA
Hoffman, William, 1937–
Queen Juliana: the story of the richest
woman in the world.
Includes index.
1. Juliana, Queen of the Netherlands, 1909–
2. Netherlands—Kings and rulers—Biography.
DJ288.H647   949.2'07'0924 [B]   79–1827
ISBN 0-15-146531-2

HBJ

First edition

B C D E

To Conrad Lynn, Eric Protter,
James Cherrier, and Patricia Hoffman

ACKNOWLEDGMENTS

Special thanks are due Michael Gillings, Donna Cherrier, Gerald Schara, Roy Vaughn, Henry Moss, Frank Aldama, David and Donna Jacobs, Donald Foster, Cordelia Herde, Mike Schneider, and George Hawley.

QUEEN
JULIANA

1

*What is war? It is the result of planetary
influences. Somewhere up there two or
three planets have approached too near to
each other.*

Pᴿᴵⁿᶜᵉˢˢ ᴹᴬᴿᴵᴶᴷᴱ, Princess Juliana's fourth daughter,
was born on February 18, 1947, but the events that would
lead perilously close to divorce and abdication did not
begin until the fall of that year. At that time Prince Bernhard, Juliana's husband, was on a hunting trip with Baron
van Heeckeren van Molecatan and was told enthusiastically
about a faith healer whose prayers had wrought miraculous cures. A member of the hunting party volunteered
that the faith healer had cured his daughter of tuberculosis, and another vouched that his blind child had been
made to see. Prince Bernhard believed the faith healer
might be the solution to what his family understandably
regarded as a tragedy.

Juliana had contracted German measles during her
pregnancy, and Marijke was born with cataracts on both
eyes. The most distinguished and expensive physicians in
the world tried to save the child's sight, but the best they
could do was restore minimal blurred vision to one eye.
The sight in the other eye was gone.

Greet Hofmans, fifty-three, faith healer, seemed an unlikely candidate to menace the stolid stability of Holland's mighty House of Orange. Greet was a pious woman, extremely polite, possessed of extraordinarily deep religious convictions. She was a stern, serious, plain-dressing, deepvoiced former Dutch factory worker who insisted God had come to her in a vision and offered supernatural powers. "Of course," said Greet Hofmans, "I accepted."

Greet Hofmans revealed that God had instructed her to move to Hattem, the baronial seat of Baron van Heeckeren van Molecatan, who became one of her earliest converts. There were other converts, and then the most important of all—Juliana—and the sober, austere Greet would end up wielding enormous influence over her powerful patron. In hushed tones she would be referred to as Holland's Rasputin; military men in Holland and NATO would detest her; Dutch industrialists would fear her; and even the orderly and democratic processes of Dutch government would come screeching to a stop. But all that came later.

It was in November 1947 that a hopeful Prince Bernhard dispatched a limousine to bring Greet Hofmans to the huge, rambling, storybook royal residence, Soestdijk Palace, for an audience with Juliana. The thin, athletic Bernhard could not have foreseen that he was placing his marriage and position of power in jeopardy.

Juliana and the faith healer spoke briefly but earnestly when they first met. Greet told Juliana she was a representative of God, that Marijke's sight could be saved if she listened to God, who spoke through Greet. Throughout Juliana's life she had been led to believe in miracles. The two women were worlds apart in upbringing, wealth, and social standing, but the religious beliefs they shared helped establish an almost immediate rapport.

Juliana was not a distinguished-looking woman. She

had a large nose and pleasant, rather homely features. She more resembled a hardy, sturdy peasant woman than a crown princess. She was tall, five feet eight, with light brown hair and blue eyes. She was a big-boned, gentle woman who long had been fascinated by astrology, mysticism, and the occult, fields of study that for years Greet Hofmans had been researching and teaching.

Juliana gave a sign and little eight-month-old Princess Marijke was carried into the large palace room. A startling, rapturous transformation came over Greet Hofmans. Suddenly she clamped her eyes shut, dropped to her knees, and launched into long, hard, fervent prayer. So unexpectedly had this occurred that at first Juliana was amazed, and then she was impressed by the faith healer's obvious piety and sincerity. Juliana had despaired of the doctors' ever helping Marijke, but perhaps this holy woman could. At last Greet Hofmans spoke: "God will give the child sight in two years if we pray hard enough."

With Bernhard's blessing, Greet Hofmans moved into Soestdijk Palace, where she divided her time by praying, helping take care of Marijke, and spiritually counseling Juliana. The facts that no scandal had ever attached to Greet's life and that her only concern seemed to be Marijke's welfare helped establish a bond of trust between her and Juliana. Each day at Soestdijk Palace there were prayer sessions attended by the entire family, often joined by Juliana's formidable mother, Queen Wilhelmina. Wilhelmina, regarded by many students of finance as the richest woman in the world (*Time* magazine estimated her personal fortune at $1 billion), was also an avid believer in astrology.

The Dutch press had hailed the marriage of Juliana and Bernhard as "The Idyll of Soestdijk," the perfect match between the dashing, charming Prince and the young,

rich Princess destined to rule all of the Netherlands; but
the marriage was hardly idyllic after Greet Hofmans arrived. Bernhard soon doubted whether he should have
allowed the mystic to move into Soestdijk Palace. Juliana
began spending increased amounts of time with Greet
Hofmans, less time with Bernhard; and it seemed to
Bernhard that his wife was developing an unhealthy de-
pendence on the faith healer.

Juliana was like any concerned mother, anxious about
her daughter's blindness and willing to cling to any
thread that promised hope, but she also was building a
relationship with Greet Hofmans that was independent of
her fears for Marijke. "You have no idea," Juliana con-
fided to Wilhelmina, "how much easier it is for me to
pray when Greet Hofmans helps me." "Greet Hofmans
has opened the way to prayer for me," Juliana happily
confessed to Baroness van Heeckeren van Molecatan.

There were other signs that alarmed Bernhard. "Miss
Hofmans," he asked, probing for the faith healer's motives, "tell me, what do you think I could do to make
better use of my life?"

The answer came right back: "You, sir, have it in you
to put Holland on the top, socially and economically,
if . . ."

Greet Hofmans was advising Bernhard to put his faith
in God, who, of course, made His intentions known
through Greet Hofmans. Bernhard, quick to anger in the
best of situations, was enraged, refused to listen to any
more, and began to think of ways to rid Soestdijk Palace
of the mystic. But Juliana was a different story altogether.
"You have it in you," Greet Hofmans told Juliana, "to
become the greatest queen Holland ever had. God has revealed this to me. But you will have to follow His
command. . . ."

Princess Juliana became Queen Juliana on September 4, 1948, when Wilhelmina abdicated after fifty years of rule. Now the Greet Hofmans connection, known only by court insiders and a few influential others, loomed much larger. Not only would Juliana inherit her mother's enormous fortune—the bulk in giant landholdings, priceless jewels and works of art, and large blocks of stock in many big corporations, the most impressive being Royal Dutch Shell—but she would head an important industrial nation and exercise powers exceeding those of most modern monarchs. As R. K. Gooch pointed out in *Governments of Continental Europe,* the Dutch sovereign plays "a role essential to parliamentary government . . . the right to be consulted, the right to encourage, the right to warn." In addition, Juliana could veto legislation by refusing to sign it.

Two years went by and Marijke's sight did not improve. The affliction worried and tormented Juliana much more than it did her child. Marijke early on showed a considerable talent for music, a talent practically nonexistent in members of the House of Orange: Wilhelmina recognized only one song, the Dutch national anthem, and that only because people stood up when it was played.

Marijke also had a talent for languages. *"Bonjour, Monsieur le Président,"* she cheerily greeted President René Coty of France.

"Formidable!" enthused the delighted French President. *"Tu parles français un peu."*

"Pas peu!" retorted Marijke angrily. *"Beaucoup!"*

Marijke's state of mind was healthy, but the Juliana-Bernhard marriage was not. Bernhard feared that Greet Hofmans might bring about a disaster economically—if Juliana began to listen to financial advice—or politically, if the faith healer began advising on affairs of state. Bern-

hard also complained that Greet Hofmans was not bringing about an improvement in his daughter's sight, but this
argument backfired. Greet Hofmans countered that the
cause of Marijke's eyesight's failing to improve was that
someone was not praying hard enough, someone was not
living a morally pure life. That someone, she intimated,
was Bernhard.

If the presence of Greet Hofmans angered and fright-
ened Bernhard, there was plenty to dismay Juliana also.
Bernhard was away from the Netherlands at least a third
of the time, on business and pleasure trips alike, and aides
delivered frequent reports on his activities to the tradition-
loving, family-oriented Juliana. As a youngster, Bernhard
had been a hell-raiser—drinking, fighting, being booted
out of Munich's Hofbräuhaus for noisy carousing—and as
an adult he turned to daredeviltry. He enjoyed racing
souped-up cars, riding fast horses, and hunting big game;
and he was almost killed in an automobile accident, a
boating mishap, and a plane crash. He broke his neck in
the automobile wreck, a one-hundred-mile-per-hour colli-
sion with a truck that occurred just ten months after his
1937 marriage to Juliana.

Greet Hofmans did not stop trying to develop a harmonious relationship with Bernhard. In 1950, more than
two years after she had moved into Soestdijk Palace, she
asked Bernhard for three hairs from the tail of his horse,
No, No, Nanette. She held the hairs in her hand, solemnly
looked skyward, and prayed to God for a message. Then
she proudly announced to a bewildered Bernhard that he
would win a place on Holland's Olympic riding team.
Bernhard's famous short temper—he once knocked some
teeth out of the mouth of a Nazi collaborator, and after
the war, when the man complained, Bernhard invited him
to the royal palace to have the rest of his teeth knocked

out—was now aimed at Greet Hofmans. Screaming, he accused her of blasphemy and demanded that she leave the palace.

Greet Hofmans did leave. In fact, her belongings were forcibly removed. Bernhard boasted that he told Juliana, "In the nation you rule; in the home, I do." But Bernhard had not scored a victory. Greet Hofmans simply moved her base of operations to former Queen Wilhelmina's estate, Het Oude Looe, where in an old gray castle surrounded by a moat she continued to minister to groups that numbered some two hundred at a time. Bankers and teachers, clergymen and lawyers, they all came to Het Oude Looe to learn that the only worthwhile relationships were those on the "vertical plane": relationships between individuals and God. "Horizontal plane" relationships, those between people, were worthless.

Juliana regularly attended the meetings at her mother's castle. She poured tea for guests, participated in discussion groups, and continued studying under Greet Hofmans and others a philosophy very similar to that propounded by the famous Russian mystic George Ivanovitch Gurdjieff (1872–1949). Gurdjieff, a former rug dealer who left Russia when the Bolsheviks took over, claimed to "heal all kinds of vices" with hypnotism, "electric emanations," and eerie dances. The religion espoused at Het Oude Looe combined conservative thinking with pacifism and mysticism and even to the present day holds a certain appeal for a few affluent members of society. The religion, following closely the tenets of Gurdjieff, held that most people were simply "mad machines," capable of great destruction but unable and unwilling to learn anything that would better them. "The distribution of knowledge," said Gurdjieff, "is based on exactly the same principle. If knowledge is given to all, nobody will get any. If it is preserved among a few, each will receive not only enough to keep, but to increase, what he receives."

Gurdjieff also believed in visitors from outer space who would advise humans if they would only "open their minds" to hear.

"What is war?" Gurdjieff once asked. "It is the result of planetary influences. Somewhere up there two or three planets have approached too near to each other."

Since war was caused by the planets, the people praying at Het Oude Looe advocated the destruction of all weapons. "Mad machines" might still wage war, but it would not be nearly so destructive.

Bernhard soon learned that his victory in removing Greet Hofmans from Soestdijk Palace was in reality a defeat. Wilhelmina was a far more stubborn adversary than the shy, introverted Juliana and was not apt to cede Bernhard any sort of rule, inside the house or out. Wilhelmina still controlled the great family fortune, and it was the money—not his marriage to the Queen of the Netherlands—that provided Bernhard's treasured ticket of admission to the highest world councils of government and finance. In addition, Wilhelmina had been annoyed with Bernhard for a number of years. Even before he married Juliana, he demanded and received a sizable yearly income from the Dutch government. Bernhard also was too often in the headlines, which did not accord with Wilhelmina's conviction that a Prince Consort should remain in the background. Finally, if Marijke's sight had not improved, Juliana's state of mind had, and Wilhelmina thought that was reason enough for Juliana to continue seeing the faith healer.

Dutch citizens were uninformed about the strange goings-on at Het Oude Looe. Newspapers in the Netherlands printed not a word about the subject, although important editors and publishers knew precisely what was happening. Later, when part of the story was revealed, they took the attitude that the affair was the personal business of the royal family and therefore not a legitimate subject for public discussion. The truth was that the Dutch press had always been extremely circumspect in divulging information that might embarrass the royal family or other powerful people in Holland, and only later would there be noticeable improvement. For obvious political and economic reasons, the press in the Netherlands, like the press in almost any other nation on earth, is reluctant to criticize the country's rulers. Meanwhile, the people of Holland remained blissfully unaware of anything's being askance in their sovereign's life.

Eleanor Roosevelt visited her wartime friend Juliana in 1951 and was almost immediately whisked to Het Oude Looe for a "Peace through Christ" meeting. Mrs. Roosevelt listened to Greet Hofmans's discourse on a number of subjects, including cancer: "A disease is not a thing in itself. Thus cancer in a person is connected with the world spiritual disorder of war. Practically speaking, therefore, I cannot cure cancer until war is eliminated." Eleanor Roosevelt could not believe what she was hearing. She attended two days of "Peace through Christ" meetings and left with grave misgivings. "I felt," she later wrote, "that it was almost arrogant to expect to establish with the Almighty a direct and conscious connection."

Yet that was what was occurring. And much more. Mrs. Roosevelt evidently did not know that the group at Het Oude Looe was trying to establish contact with the space visitors Gurdjieff had talked about.

Bernhard's position was precarious. Baron van Heeckeren van Molecatan, descended from old-line feudal nobility, one of Greet Hofmans's first converts, had been installed as Juliana's private secretary, and van Heeckeren van Molecatan's mother had become grand mistress at court. The two were soon the dominant voices in the court, even helping convert Juliana's ladies-in-waiting to their brand of mysticism. Bernhard was frustrated, isolated, and ignored. It was in the court where the great decisions of monarchy were made, and Bernhard was almost totally shut out from that court, which consisted of aging nobility totally dedicated to their Queen.

One of the leaders at Het Oude Looe was J. W. Kaiser, a thin, fervent man with burning eyes and unbending beliefs. His Gurdjieffist type of pacifism appealed to Juliana. And had not Christ Himself been a pacifist? On a 1952 state visit to the United States, Juliana penciled some remarks onto speeches written for her by ministers, remarks that could be interpreted as urging the Netherlands to disarm and to steer a neutral course in the Cold War. Dutch Foreign Minister Dirk U. Stikker literally begged the Queen not to deliver the controversial statements, and what could have triggered a national crisis in the Netherlands was averted. Nevertheless, in many of Juliana's speeches there were vague references to mysticism, and during her address before a joint session of the United States Congress she called for more spending on social needs and less on defense. "Let us do the best we can," she concluded. "Leave the rest to God."

Holland's influential *Het Parool* made it clear what it thought of Juliana's performance but avoided directly criticizing the Queen by saying it assumed the speeches had been written by ministers. The speeches, editorialized *Het Parool,* had the ring of "views hailed by pacifists, 'third way' people and some mystics. . . . Do they hear voices in The Hague and are they haunted by visions? . . . Doubtless these speeches are well-intentioned. . . . Nevertheless we realize with painful embarrassment . . . that all of this might leave the impression that Holland is a queer country."

The *Het Parool* editorial was clearly meant for Juliana's eyes, but the newspaper would learn, as Bernhard already had, that the Queen of the Netherlands would not back down when religion was concerned.

Bernhard was on the board of directors of numerous important corporations, including the Royal Blast Furnaces and Steel Factories in Velsen, KLM (Royal Dutch Airlines), and Fokker Aircraft, and he shared with his hardheaded fellow directors the conviction that Juliana was terribly misguided, that Holland needed to spend *more* for defense, not less. Earlier Bernhard had been instrumental in persuading KLM to purchase Douglas DC-8 jets. While in the United States in 1952, he found time to journey to California and test-fly Lockheed's newest airplane, an airplane he was soon urging European industry to buy. As Inspector General of the Netherlands Armed Forces and a member of the National Council of Defense, Bernhard's voice was crucial when deciding which war planes Holland would need.

All of these activities were contingent on Bernhard's remaining married to the Dutch Queen, but the matter was personally humiliating as well. He was responsible for a strong national defense and his wife was calling for disarmament. About all Bernhard could do was complain bitterly about the people with whom Juliana had surrounded herself. But Juliana had complaints of her own, and when she heard what Bernhard was saying, she struck back. Many of Bernhard's friends and business associates, she pointed out, had rather checkered pasts. Among them were wheeler-dealer fast-buck entrepreneurs, international playboys, and even former Nazis. This sort of marital hostility led to a dead end, and Bernhard proposed a deal to Juliana. He would abandon his friends if she would stop seeing hers. Juliana thought long and hard about the arrangement. An international scandal ending in divorce, conflict between the Crown and the government—these were events that conceivably could bring down even the powerful House of Orange. But in the end Juliana let her conscience and heart rule instead of common sense, which might have suggested she put the throne first. "No, Bernilo," she finally said, "I don't believe that is the solution."

The royal couple grew farther apart. Seldom were they seen together, and when they were, the result was more often than not embarrassing. Bernhard openly snubbed his wife at a banquet by leaving her to sit alone, a major breach of royal etiquette, and Juliana pointedly turned on her heels and walked away from her husband during a television appearance at Schiphol Airport. Juliana refused to attend Bernhard's birthday party, one of the top social occasions on the calendar. The shaky marriage was complicated by Juliana's suspicion that Bernhard maintained mistresses in several cities abroad.

Juliana continued to alarm the Dutch government by making remarks that seemed to call for pacifism. Bernhard seized upon some of his wife's statements to launch a desperate campaign to rescue his floundering marriage. He leaked the story of Greet Hofmans and Het Oude Looe to West Germany's *Time*-style weekly newsmagazine, the 250,000-circulation *Der Spiegel,* and soon much of the world was talking about the "female Rasputin" and her fabulously rich sponsor.

But not that part of the world that included Holland. This was June 1956, more than *eight years* after Greet Hofmans had entered the royal family's life, and still the nation's newspapers were resorting to censorship. Nervous

Dutch editors, encouraged by prominent members of government and the business community, continued to sit on the story. The later explanation that the story was withheld to protect privacy rings false. It seems Greet Hofmans was so influential that she was telling Juliana what bills she should and should not sign into law, a revelation that certainly overrode any rights to personal privacy. In any case, the news blackout was clumsy and inevitably doomed to fail in a country as open as Holland once *Der Spiegel* had broken the story. Tourists brought the news into the country—author Geoffrey Bocca was one of the first to tell Americans—and the Dutch people starting snapping up foreign newspapers, standing in long lines to grab them as soon as they arrived. Some papers sold for more than $5 each. Eager citizens gathered in parks and on street corners to read and discuss the news. English newspapers attacked the Netherlands for a "conspiracy of silence," and Dutch officials accused the British of "bad taste." Numerous other countries, including the United States, began to poke fun at the Netherlands.

It was a number of days after the rest of the world had learned of the scandal before the people of the Netherlands could read about the story in their own newspapers, and even then some of the more fascinating details were omitted. At an unusual press conference for sixty foreign journalists, Prime Minister Willem Drees, whose Socialists had just won the national elections in the Netherlands, said there was "no question of abdication." He emphasized that what Greet Hofmans was doing was legal and admitted that Juliana was still seeing her. In fact, Dutch legal officials had considered embarrassing Juliana by charging Greet with practicing medicine without a license, but this turned out not to be feasible because the faith healer had not charged for her services.

Also, despite what Prime Minister Drees said, there

was a great deal of talk about abdication. It was on the tongues of almost everyone in the country, from Juliana on down. "The royal example," editorialized the prestigious *Haagse Post,* "can easily contribute to the fostering of quackery." The Calvinist *Trouw,* a strongly royalist newspaper, declared, "We are filled with deep concern." Nonetheless, some newsmen who worked for these papers at the time concede that their managements were worried about leaping into the fray on either side. It was not clear whether Bernhard would win, or Juliana, or for that matter if either would emerge on top.

Juliana's oldest daughter, eighteen-year-old Crown Princess Beatrix, was next in line for the throne, and Beatrix sided with Bernhard. The teenage Princess had always been more attracted to her dashing father than to her rather plain, very religious mother, and it is not impossible that her selection of Bernhard was also influenced by what she herself obviously stood to gain. Rumors swept the Netherlands that Beatrix would soon be Queen, and the rumors were lent credence when Prime Minister Drees, at the peak of the crisis, praised her as "a very sensible girl." Emotions heated even more when one of Juliana's closest advisers accused Bernhard of plotting to force his wife's abdication in the belief he would exercise more power in a regime headed by his daughter. Bernhard was unavailable for comment, having journeyed to Stockholm to watch the equestrian Olympics.

A majority of the Dutch people supported Juliana. Most people in Holland wanted the monarchy, felt they needed it, feared that turmoil and chaos might result without it. Women particularly believed Juliana had acted in a very human manner, seeking help for Marijke from every possible source. But Dutch citizens also resented the German connection exemplified by German-born Bernhard and *Der Spiegel*. Some of them had taken to the streets twenty years before to protest the announcement of Juliana's engagement to Bernhard, and many more recalled the German invasion that began on May 10, 1940, and devastated their country.

Although elections had just been held, Dutch officials refused to form a government until the Greet Hofmans problem was resolved. Partly it was a matter of self-preservation. "The King is inviolable," reads the Dutch Constitution; "the ministers are responsible." This meant that no matter what Juliana commanded, she was blameless, but the minister who carried out her order might lay himself open to all kinds of prosecutions. If the minister refused to carry out one of Juliana's commands, Juliana could dismiss the minister and find another, but again that minister would be held accountable by the state. In sum, Juliana had total immunity and by law could command literally anything. In practice, of course, her power was tempered by political realities that necessitated compromise with other powerful elements of society, but in the Netherlands of 1956 no one was willing to step forward and find out what those "tempering" elements might do. The problem was compounded by the tremendous wealth, power, and prestige of former Queen Wilhelmina standing foursquare behind her only daughter and heir. "If someone doesn't take some action soon," predicted a government official who chose to remain anonymous, "you can be sure that we'll soon have both divorce and abdication."

Juliana was determined to avoid abdication. She did not want Beatrix to assume the throne, a move she suspected would not be unacceptable either to her daughter or to Bernhard. Juliana had been required by the Dutch Constitution to obtain permission from the government for her marriage, but the Constitution said nothing about divorce or abdication, and it certainly said nothing about abdication *after* divorce. She had the law in her corner, and most of the people in Holland besides. But still the situation was intolerable. Modern, dynamic, industrialized Holland was a nation without a government, and so it seemed destined to remain unless the Greet Hofmans crisis could be resolved and ministers could be found who were willing to serve.

It was late in June 1956 when Juliana agreed to the appointment of three elder statesmen, soon to be called "the three wise men," who would "investigate" the royal problem and "counsel" the Queen and her husband. In fact, the three men—former Premier Pieter S. Gerbrandy, former Vice-Premier L. J. M. Beel, and permanent NATO delegate A. W. L. van Starkenborgh Stachouwer—intended either to reconcile the marriage or to arrange the smooth transition of Beatrix to the throne.

For two months there was little news about the delicate negotiations. Finally, late in August, the royal couple released a brief communiqué saying simply that the three wise men "have reported their findings to us and given us advice. Their advice has been a very valuable contribution to the solution of difficulties which had arisen. We now look forward to the future with confidence."

The communication itself said little enough, but insiders with experience interpreting such messages immediately assured the world the crisis was ended. The press in Holland and abroad reported that Juliana would see no more of Greet Hofmans, attend no more religious meetings at Het Oude Looe, and that Baron van Heeckeren van Molecatan and his mother were on their way out of the royal court. Even the objective signs of a settlement were favorable. The heir presumptive, Beatrix, left the royal palace to study at the University of Leyden, indicating that no abdication was in the offing. Juliana and Bernhard flew to Corfu for a vacation with the Greek royal family, a vacation one Amsterdam newspaper described as an "interlude in the land of classical harmony and joy of living" that spelled "the equally harmonious conclusion of a difficult period."

But matters really were not resolved at all; in fact, they were worsened. Juliana read the newspaper accounts and was outraged. They seemed to detail a complete capitulation on her part, which was not at all what she had understood in agreeing to the communiqué. Anyone reading it could see that. First, she had not agreed to stop seeing Greet Hofmans. Second, she had not consented to dismiss key members of her court. Finally, she would never agree to abandon her religious beliefs. All of the stories were lies, designed, she believed, to pressure her into doing what the civil authorities wanted. Juliana might be introverted and withdrawn, but she was also proud and she especially resented the implication that a Queen of the House of Orange, answerable to no earthly power, had been forced to make humiliating promises to three civilian advisers.

Again Juliana was supported by Wilhelmina. The crafty former Queen may have been alarmed by the continuous whittling away of royal power, in both the Netherlands and other countries, and believed this was the time—with the people supporting the monarch—to make a stand.

Juliana continued her visits to the religious gatherings at Het Oude Looe and let it be known that she was still seeing Greet Hofmans. The politics of Holland were turned upside down: a number of Dutch leftists found themselves defending the Queen in her "fight against the militarists," and rightists who normally supported the monarchy resumed their calls for abdication. There were also prominent Dutch citizens who just wished the whole mess would go away. Some had attended meetings at Wilhelmina's castle, hoping by their presence to impress Juliana, while others genuinely believed Greet Hofmans had special powers. Neither category of person wanted the story to proceed any further.

It often seemed in private conversations that the Netherlands was fast becoming a laughingstock. Powerful Dutch businessmen endured rounds of jokes about strange, other-world figures advising their Queen. These businessmen wanted it stopped; the Holland of 1956 was not Russia in 1916. But then two of the three wise men made the situation worse by claiming publicly that Juliana had gone back on her word.

This was more than the Queen of the Netherlands could take. She threatened to appear on nationwide television and radio to explain her position to her subjects, an act that Prime Minister Willem Drees believed would be unseemly and ludicrous. Drees issued an order to broadcasting authorities forbidding them to allow Juliana on the air. Forbidding a sovereign to talk to her subjects was almost unprecedented, but it was an order supported by both Bernhard and Beatrix. There also was fear that Juliana, a simple but effective speaker, might carry the day if she was allowed to go before the people of the Netherlands.

At last there was a sufficient consensus in powerful Dutch political and business circles to apply heavy pressure on Juliana. If she would not remove herself or make concessions, she would have to be removed, no matter how unpopular such an action might be. A modern state just could not function with a Rasputin behind the scenes. What ensued was a fierce, largely unpublicized power struggle that neither side really won in the end.

A permanent government was finally formed and Juliana, albeit more discreetly, continued to pray with her friends at Het Oude Looe. The dangers to Juliana, indeed to the House of Orange, were that Parliament might have amended the Constitution to provide for forced abdication, a solution few people in the nation wanted, or that it might have abolished monarchy in the Netherlands altogether, an even less popular answer. As it was, Juliana survived, but in the future her speeches and public pronouncements would be closely monitored by a nervous government that wanted to hear nothing more about the religious imperative of disarmament.

The marriage to Bernhard, most people in Holland agreed, was nothing more than a masquerade, but Princess Marijke, whose blindness had been the catalyst for the affair, surprised everyone with her progress. Her eyesight had improved with medically supervised treatment and exercises to the point where she could safely ride a bicycle in traffic, and in every way she seemed a pleasant, ordinary little girl.

Greet Hofmans faded from the public eye. She was simply shown the door, thrown out. Nevertheless, Juliana could never be persuaded to denounce the stern, solemn faith healer, who died in obscurity in 1968.

Juliana herself, without compromising her beliefs, came through a tremendous political storm. She had done nothing wrong in her own eyes or in those of her subjects, but most impressive was her ability to endure, to cling to what she had against powerful opposition that demanded nothing less than her public destruction.

Yet Juliana's endurance should not have been surprising. It was a trait possessed by her illustrious ancestors, and by the remarkable House of Orange itself.

2

The Constitution need not be more than
a toy in the hands of the people, so that
they enjoy the illusion of freedom, whereas
in reality we knead them as circumstances
shall require.

THE ENDURING House of Orange-Nassau, to which Queen Juliana belongs, was created in 1544 through the merging of two noble families, Orange and Nassau. The House of Nassau itself began in 1159 when Count Walram of Laurenburg took the name Walram of Nassau, after Nassau Castle in western Germany where he lived. One of Walram's descendants, William of Nassau, inherited the title Prince of Orange in 1544 from his cousin, René of Chalons. William of Nassau, who became known as William the Silent, was one of the sixteenth century's most important figures: he was the founder of the modern Dutch nation, the "Father of the Fatherland."

The father of William the Silent was William the Rich, and his mother was Juliana of Stolberg, after whom Queen Juliana would be named more than three and a half centuries later. Part of the very real affection the Dutch people today feel for Juliana is derived from the fact that she is descended from the family that led and won the war of independence from Spain. "The House of Orange protects us," is a fervent statement heard over and over again, not just in the poorer sections of Amsterdam and Rotterdam, but in villages and farming communities as well. A similar situation might exist in the United States if a current descendant of George Washington ruled the country, and if throughout the nation's history most of its leaders had been blood descendants of Washington.

The war for independence against Spain lasted *eighty* years, and the House of Orange did indeed play a heroic role in the victory. Three brothers of William the Silent gave their lives: Adolph died in the very first battle, in 1569; Lodewijk and Hendrik were killed on a battlefield near Mook. William the Silent himself was not spared. He became the first Stadtholder (Governor) of the newly declared Dutch Republic in 1579, but was assassinated in 1584 by Spanish agents and was succeeded as Stadtholder by his son, Maurice. It was Maurice who succeeded in driving the Spanish soldiers out of the provinces that now comprise the Netherlands.

The Dutch war of independence has often been portrayed as a struggle for religious freedom from Catholic Spain, and many people did participate for that undeniably just cause. The ultimate fight, however, was between nascent, dynamic capitalism and outmoded feudalism. Many in the "merchant" class who sided with William the Silent were in reality pirates who had learned to eke out a living sailing the seas. Their expertise, and that of their descendants, was to prove invaluable in the 1602 formation of the Dutch East India Company, whose incredibly profitable operation became the envy of much of the world. Of course, members of the House of Orange participated in the great wealth accumulated by the East India Company. The House of Orange not only was Holland's leading political family, it was the leading financial family. The glory and wealth of the Netherlands, gathered by the efforts of many, were credited in many instances to the farsighted policies of the ruling family. Today the House of Orange still rules the country, Juliana is the nation's wealthiest citizen, and considerable credit and sincere devotion is given her.

The Dutch East India Company really was a marvel. The company founded and consolidated, in less than fifty years, a vast overseas empire, a small part of which still acknowledges Juliana as its sovereign. The East India Company sent its ships around the world, returning to Holland with riches far beyond the dreams of feudal kings. The company gained economic *and* political control in much of India and Indonesia, the Cape of Good Hope, and Ceylon. It employed the harshest and most brutal methods of colonial exploitation, including the widespread use of slave labor, and from the beginning demonstrated a marked racial consciousness that even today is seen in South Africa. Natives in many cases simply were not considered human. However, the people who controlled the East India Company differed from their counterparts in Spain and Portugal in that they had no desire to thrust their religious beliefs on those they were colonizing. The Dutch were businessmen, not missionaries. Thus, while much of South America is Catholic, the tenets of Calvinism never took hold in Indonesia.

Whenever Juliana visits the United States, she can count on a big and joyous welcome from Dutch-Americans. It was the Dutch East India Company, only seven years after its formation, that sent Henry Hudson up New York Bay in 1609. In 1614 the Dutch States-General (Parliament) gave the East India Company a monopoly for fur trade in New Netherland, which was all land between Virginia and Canada. A year later came the first Dutch settlement on Manhattan Island, in 1623 New Netherland formally became a Dutch colony, and in 1626 Manhattan was bought from the Indians for products worth $24.

It is not simply the early economic success of Holland that Juliana's subjects can associate with the House of Orange, but tremendous, perhaps unprecedented cultural achievements. A visitor to the Netherlands still hears about the nation's Golden Age—roughly 1600 to 1680—when the great talents of the Dutch people, unshackled at last from imprisoning feudalism, burst forth into a mighty bloom, as do the country's beautiful and famous flowers. The names still live in history: Rembrandt, Van Dyck, Rubens, Cuyp, Vermeer, Hals, so many others. Probably no country in the world produced so many great artists in so short a time. Yet, as University of Amsterdam Professor Paul Zumthor pointed out, "In the eyes of the aristocracy and the wealthy bourgeoisie the painter was a supplier of goods like any other." Almost every great Dutch artist of the period died penniless.

The Dutch Republic's third House of Orange Stadtholder in the ancestral line that would lead to Juliana was Frederick Henry, who came to power in 1625 when his half brother Maurice died. Frederick Henry is remembered as the "Conqueror of Cities" because of his scientific application of siege warfare to capture urban centers from the Spanish, and because of the widespread, almost monumental, nepotism and corruption that flourished during his rule. When Frederick Henry died in 1647, the Peace of Munster, ending eighty years of war, was only a year away.

William II, son of Frederick Henry, ruled for only three years, 1647–1650, and when he died the States-General, representing the country's merchant class, decided the Dutch could get along without a Stadtholder. Business in the colonies was lucrative and there was fear that a

Stadtholder might demand too great a tribute from the profits of the merchants. The States-General, ruling in behalf of business, took control of the nation. Even today in the Netherlands, although of course the misconception is much more prevalent in other countries, there are people who believe that Juliana descends from a House of Orange that has ruled continuously since the time of William the Silent.

The States-General that took power after William II in 1650 was a body such as perhaps had never before been seen in history. It was a group composed largely of capitalists, without even the bother of a pretense like putting up a king or popular politician as a figurehead. The Dutch East India and other such companies, which never tried to rationalize policy with religion, took over as straightforwardly at home as they had abroad.

It did not take long for the States-General to learn that it could only rule effectively when the affairs of the nation were running smoothly. Successive wars with France and England demonstrated that quarreling factions within the ruling body could not provide the centralized leadership necessary for the country's defense. What was good for one business concern might not be good for another, and even within individual companies there was disagreement over the best policies to pursue. Needed was someone making decisions who "stood above the battle," a function that today is considered one of Juliana's most important.

Twenty-two-year-old William III, son of William II, was named Stadtholder in 1672. The urban bourgeoisie in the Netherlands were still not willing to trust the title of King to anyone, so fresh were their memories of the hated Spanish monarchs, but the man they appointed Stadtholder would become much more than just the King of Holland. His triumphs would become part of the legend of the House of Orange, a legacy embodied now in Juliana.

William III of Orange led armies that repelled the invading English and French, and his admirals, Tromp and DeRuyter, won important victories at sea. But the greatest triumph of William III came in 1688 when much of England was demanding the overthrow of the House of Stuart headed by the autocratic James II, a Catholic. In June 1688 influential figures in the English church and state invited William III to intervene, and on November 5, with 24,000 men, he landed at Torbay. It was a gamble that paid off and changed history. The wind that swept Holland's William III into England held the British fleet on the shore.

There was not much of a fight. James II was a tyrant, a Catholic besides, and many in England welcomed William III as a liberator. James II fled but was captured and sent back to London. He later was allowed to escape to France where an army was mobilized: the army was defeated at the Battle of the Boyne in 1690 and the luckless James II lived out his last years in France.

William III was married to Mary Stuart, the daughter of James II, and this relationship gave legitimacy to his claim to the British throne. History records, however, that this was a rare period of dual monarchs: William *and* Mary. Nevertheless, it was a source of irony for all those who followed William III in the House of Orange, including Juliana, that when the Dutch people would call him only Stadtholder, the mighty British Empire called him King. Not only that, he was a very important King.

The victory of William III assured the success of what is known as the Glorious Revolution, and it continued the historically important beginning of the transition in England from personal monarchy to constitutional monarchy. William III, despite assertions by some historians to the contrary, hated the English Parliament—for obvious reasons he also hated the Dutch States-General—and his main reason for acknowledging its authority was so that he could secure money and supplies for his armies. After the victory of William III, English monarchs increasingly would have to petition Parliament for approval of their actions.

The reign of William and Mary was not entirely progressive. It fell short in the area of religious freedom guarantees, an area in which the House of Orange, straight through the reign of Juliana, has been rightly praised. England's Toleration Act of 1689 did not bestow citizenship rights on Catholics or Protestant Nonconformists, which was not surprising since William III had been asked to invade England to overthrow a Catholic king. Catholics were arbitrarily and vigorously persecuted in England under William III, a policy he assented to because his overriding goal was the enlistment of English help in the struggle to contain Catholic France and Louis XIV. In this he succeeded: what followed was more than a century of war between England and France that did not end until Napoleon's defeat at Waterloo.

William III died childless in 1702. Mary was already dead, so William III was succeeded on the English throne by Anne, Mary's younger sister. But the House of Orange lost more than just the English throne. Once again the Dutch States-General decided the nation could prosper without a member of the House of Orange as Stadtholder. As in the past, it was the specter of a powerful leader taking too much for his services that prompted wealthy Dutch businessmen to try to manage on their own through the instrument of the States-General. The fear of too much power in the hands of a single individual was enlarged when the businessmen pondered the enormous power William III had gathered. Just as important, the amazing Dutch East India Company, returning huge dividends to investors—36 percent annually between 1713 and 1722—and other burgeoning Dutch companies possessed such great financial strength that it seemed possible to survive on their own.

It was not possible. Just as William III was called upon during a time of war, another conflict, this time the War of the Austrian Succession, threatened the independence of the Netherlands, and it was necessary to find centralized leadership to unite the squabbling factions against the danger from outside. The States-General selected the House of Orange in the form of William IV, the descendant of a brother of William the Silent. Thus, when Juliana's subjects look upon her and the House of Orange as their protectors, they have a great deal of history on their side. William the Silent freed the country from Spanish persecution. William III preserved the nation during a perilous period. Now William IV would do the same.

William IV was popular among the masses, who blamed the ruling businessmen for their plight. Despite the economic success of Dutch enterprises, most people were impoverished. William IV was in a powerful position, and before being declared Stadtholder in 1747 he was able to extract important concessions from the States-General. His function (Stadtholder) was made hereditary, and he was appointed Director-General of the Dutch East India Company. William IV guided the nation through the war, but in other respects his rule fell short of popular expectations. Adriaan J. Barnouw wrote, in *The Pageant of Netherlands History:* "Unfortunately, Prince William IV was not the kind of man to make good use of the almost dictatorial power that was thrust upon him. His timorous mind was suspicious of popular movements. A conservative by nature, he felt a closer affinity to the privileged class that had barred him from power than to the masses to which he owed it."

When William IV died at age forty in 1751, he was succeeded by his son, the three-year-old William V. The new Stadtholder would turn out not to be a strong leader, but he ruled during a period of Holland's decline as a world power. His government is best remembered for its close ties with the newly independent United States, for a disastrous war with England (1780–1784), and for its inability to cope with the powerful revolutionary tide spilling out of France. In 1776 the Netherlands was the first country to recognize the new American nation, and in 1779 Captain John Paul Jones was given a hero's reception in Amsterdam. This policy, disastrous for Holland, was conceived by powerful Dutch merchants who sought to profit from England's loss in the New World. Instead it led to a war with Great Britain that the Dutch could not hope to win, and much of the nation was left destitute and angry. William V had an explanation for the Dutch defeat: "In the last century, the wages which the common man could earn were generally lower, the population was greater and poverty was more widespread than at present; and so it was easier to enlist men for the sea service." But this explanation was mistaken. As Charles R. Boxer pointed out in *The Dutch Seaborne Empire: 1600–1800,* "It was one of the stock complaints of writers of the decade 1770–80, that unemployment and poverty in the United Provinces were probably more serious and widespread than at any time since the Treaty of Munster."

The defeat by England created a class of determined young revolutionaries that William V decided to handle with force. This was a grave mistake. William V was married to the sister of the King of Prussia, whom he persuaded to attack the anti-Orangists. Thousands of these people escaped to Paris, "the university of revolution and patriotism," in 1787, and when they returned in 1795 it was with a French army. William V was forced to flee to England. In the same year the Dutch East India Company, besieged by corruption, declared bankruptcy, and only in the next century would the company's colonial empire be picked up by other Dutch financial interests.

As happened twice before, and would happen again one more time, the chain of rule that connects Juliana to William the Silent was broken. This time the break was much more serious. Previously the Dutch people had preferred rule by the House of Orange to that of the merchants, but in 1795 the returning radicals and their French escort were greeted as saviors. Only later, when Napoleon appointed his brother Louis Bonaparte as King, did popular discontent begin to appear. Fifteen thousand young Dutch soldiers were forced to march with Napoleon into Russia, and only a few hundred managed to straggle home to recount the horrors of their experience.

When Napoleon was defeated for the final time at Waterloo, the Viennese Congress annexed Belgium to the Netherlands as a bulwark against the French, and William I, the son of William V, began in 1815 the modern reign of the House of Orange in Holland. He was called William I because he was King, not a Stadtholder as his ancestors had been. William I was the great-great-grandfather of Juliana.

Ironically, it was the reign of King Louis Bonaparte that paved the way for the acceptance of William I as King. Louis Bonaparte's reign, although corrupt, had been a mild one, notable for its lack of extreme repression, and it was his relative leniency that prompted his brother, Emperor Napoleon, to take a more direct role in governing the Netherlands. It was the memory of Louis Bonaparte that softened the historic Dutch fear of kings.

William I was the absolute ruler of Holland, and soon he was disliked by almost everyone in the country. His sole support came from the wealthier section of the merchant community, which found no cause for dissatisfaction with a King who was himself a businessman. And, indeed, business was once again booming, with William I increasing a personal fortune that one day would find its way to Juliana. The cause for the business boom was that the Netherlands was steadily picking up the pieces of its old colonial empire.

The Netherlands had a constitution, but William I did not take it seriously. "The constitution," he said, "need not be more than a toy in the hands of the people, whereas in reality we knead them as circumstances shall require."

The people of Belgium revolted against the rule of William I, burning down much of Brussels, and other European powers granted the nation independence in 1830 under the leadership of Prince Leopold of Saxe-Coburg-Gotha—King Leopold. William I led an army into Belgium, but the combined strength of Austria, France, Great Britain, Prussia, and Russia, all of whom supported King Leopold, persuaded him to withdraw.

William I, still smarting from the loss of Belgium (he did not recognize its independence until 1839), abdicated in 1840 and was succeeded on the throne by his son William II. It was the continuation by William II of his father's autocratic policies that finally led to major reform in the Netherlands. The reforms were the result of efforts by the cautious, but persistent and increasingly powerful, Liberal Party, which realized that change would come either peacefully or violently, but come it would. There was famine in the Netherlands in the 1840s, which led to a massive immigration to America's Middle West, and the potential for social upheaval was great. In 1848 William II was forced to accept constraints on his power, constraints that forever altered and weakened the power of the Dutch monarchy and formed the essential framework under which, even today, Juliana reigns.

William III, the last of the Dutch Kings, came to the throne in 1849. His main political support derived from the Anti-Revolutionary Party, a coalition of conservative monarchists who openly proclaimed that they were op-posed to "the rationalism of the eighteenth century." William III fought the ideas of the Liberal Party as best he could, but the tide of history and the objective need of Holland to modernize were too much to overcome. In his last years he became less interested in opposing change and more concerned with assuring the continuation of the House of Orange.

The House of Orange, that is, the branch represented by William III, was on the verge of dying out. Three sons had been born to William III, but he outlived them all. At age sixty-two, however, in 1879, William III married for a second time. His wife was Princess Emma of Waldeck-Pyrmont, and on August 31, 1880, Juliana's mother, the future Queen Wilhelmina, was born.

RULERS OF
THE NETHERLANDS

YEARS	OFFICE	NAME
1579–1584	Stadtholder	William the Silent
1584–1625	Stadtholder	Maurice
1625–1647	Stadtholder	Frederick Henry
1647–1650	Stadtholder	William II
1650–1672	Country governed by States-General	
1672–1702	Stadtholder	William III
1702–1747	Country governed by States-General	
1747–1751	Stadtholder	William IV
1751–1795	Stadtholder	William V
1795–1815	Country governed by France	
1815–1840	King	William I
1840–1849	King	William II
1849–1890	King	William III
1890–1940	Queen	Wilhelmina
1940–1945	Country governed by Germany	
1945–1948	Queen	Wilhelmina
1948–	Queen	Juliana

3

The archenemy of mankind, Adolf Hitler,
has tried to annihilate us.

THEY THOUGHT of Wilhelmina as a man. "We will maintain your inviolability and your rights as King," the President of the States-General told her. "She is the greatest man on the throne today," said an admiring English diplomat during World War I. "The only King in Europe," said a French diplomat during the Second World War, "is the Queen of the Netherlands." Wilhelmina even thought of herself as a man. "I swear," she said, taking the oath at her inauguration, "that I will defend the independence of the country as a good King should."

Wilhelmina became Queen of the Netherlands at age ten in 1890, but her mother, Queen Emma, served as Regent until 1898. Emma was a conservative, no-nonsense woman firmly committed to the principles and privileges of monarchy, and Wilhelmina was raised in what she later described as "The Cage": an isolated, lonely, formal, friendless atmosphere that barred her from even the most minimal contact with her future subjects. The Cage Wilhelmina so often sadly referred to left an indelible stamp on her character. The world would come to regard her as stern and cold, aloof and humorless, but there was a cut of greatness in her.

Wilhelmina's entire childhood was a preparation for later responsibilities. Brilliant educators gave her private lessons in constitutional law, history, and languages. Holland's most important admirals and generals came to the royal palace to ground her in the fundamentals of military science, and the finest economics instructors filled her head with the intricacies of finance. Bible study and a thorough grounding in religion completed her curriculum, none of which had been left to chance. Wilhelmina did *not* read children's books, nor did she romp in sandboxes with playmates, and later, regretting what she had missed, she would try hard to make things different for Juliana.

Occasionally Wilhelmina would try a minor revolt against the rigid discipline imposed by Emma, but the result was most often simply comical. Once Wilhelmina wanted to play with her dolls, but Emma had something else planned. "If I don't get my way," said the future Queen, "I'll go out on the balcony and tell my subjects."

Queen Emma could not have known, as she charted her daughter's future, about the almost literal mountain of money atop which Wilhelmina would one day sit. She would be rich, yes, with great holdings in land, jewels, art, the accumulated inheritance of the House of Orange—that was why she studied economics—but who could have known that she would become the richest woman in the world, that her wealth would rival that of any Rothschild or Rockefeller? Yet even as Wilhelmina studied, a tiny company named Royal Dutch, founded by a trader named Jean Kessler, was granted a royal charter in 1890. Kessler enlisted the aid of a bookkeeper named Henri Deterding and a merchant, Hugo Loudon; and thanks in large measure to the oil-saturated Dutch East Indies they were able to escape the fate that befell so many similar operations: annihilation by Standard Oil. Eventually, Royal Dutch merged with Britain's Shell, 60 percent of the new company in Dutch hands, to form what is now the colossal Royal Dutch Shell, the largest industrial corporation outside the United States and the third largest in the world. This mighty profit-generating machine today has assets that are greater than the entire gross national products of all but a handful of nations, and in on the ground floor, the *royal* in Royal Dutch Shell, was the House of Orange in the person of young Queen Wilhelmina.

The same year Royal Dutch received its charter, 1890, ten-year-old Wilhelmina stood on the balcony of the royal palace in Amsterdam and looked down upon a cheering throng of subjects. "Mama," she asked Emma, "do all these people belong to me?"

"No, my child," said Emma. "It is you who belong to all these people."

Wilhelmina had plenty of spunk even as a little girl. She once visited Germany's powerful Kaiser Wilhelm. "See," said the Kaiser, "my guards are seven feet tall and yours are only shoulder high to them."

"Quite true, Your Majesty," piped back Wilhelmina, "your guards are seven feet tall. But when we open our dikes, the water is ten feet deep."

One of Wilhelmina's first trips abroad occurred when she journeyed to England at age thirteen as a guest of Queen Victoria. What a meeting it was! The aging symbol of nineteenth-century monarchy meeting the child many regard as her twentieth-century counterpart. They would be responsible for forming two of the world's great fortunes: that held by Juliana, and that of Queen Elizabeth of England. The two also would leave lasting imprints on their respective nations.

Wilhelmina was asked what impressed her most about Great Britain. "Oh, your policemen! They were wonderful. And the pipers at Windsor! But most of all your Queen Victoria. She took me for a drive and I've never seen anyone sit so straight. I couldn't believe she was smaller than me."

Wilhelmina was "invested" as Queen in 1898 in the New Church in Amsterdam, the fourth monarch and eleventh member of the House of Orange to rule the Netherlands, but the first woman. In fact, a special law had been passed to permit her to assume the throne. Characteristically, Wilhelmina was not awed by the occasion. Custom dictated that the Prime Minister write her speech, but the teenage Queen insisted on composing her own. Before a surprised assemblage that included the representatives of many governments of the world, Wilhelmina delivered what was reported to be her own speech. Many guests raised their eyebrows at the balls, parties, and receptions that ensued, but the fact was that Wilhelmina would outlast almost all of them.

Only two years after becoming Queen, Wilhelmina moved boldly on the international scene. She ordered the Dutch warship *Gelderland* to South Africa to rescue the embattled President of the Transvaal, Paul Kruger, who was leading an insurrection against the British. The *Gelderland* defied an English naval blockade to bring Kruger to asylum in Holland. "Among all the kings," wrote the French poet Jean Rameau, "only you made a manly gesture."

Wilhelmina was married in 1900 to Henry, Duke of Mecklenburg-Schwerin, who filled the Dutch constitutional requirement of being Protestant. Henry was denied

the title of Prince of the Netherlands, was denied anything approaching a significant income from the state,
and found a certain satisfaction in hobbies and his one
honorary position as president of the Dutch Red Cross.

Prince Henry already had become almost a legend in
the Netherlands. He is reported to have been burdened
with child payments for the several offspring he fathered
outside marriage, and there are still taxi drivers who remember the police pouring him into their cabs outside
nightclubs for the ride back to the royal palace. In later
years Henry enjoyed chatting and drinking with the
exiled Kaiser Wilhelm, and he evidently had a sharp eye
for chambermaids and royalty alike.

Wilhelmina tolerated Prince Henry's shenanigans, say
people in Holland, because they kept him out of the way.
It mattered, however, that he be thought of as president
of the Dutch Red Cross.

The young Queen of the Netherlands did not intend to
preside over the dismantling of the Dutch colonial empire
any more than she proposed to witness the further erosion
of the power of the House of Orange. Her own great
wealth was tied into that empire, and she agreed with the
essential rightness of monarchy. Most important, Wilhelmina had considerable abilities that she brought to her
task, abilities far exceeding those of her immediate prede-
cessors on the Dutch throne. One of Wilhelmina's more
impressive accomplishments was keeping the Netherlands
neutral and out of European wars until forced to fight by
Hitler; but she was not averse—when Dutch economic
interests were involved—to committing military might to
actions in Turkey and India, to siding with England and
the United States over the annexation of Mexican oil
properties, and to skirmishing with oil-rich Venezuela
over the Dutch West Indies. But her efforts in behalf of a

European peace were truly monumental, and had more rulers possessed her foresight, the world might not have been plunged so precipitately into the senseless slaughter of World War I. Just one year after her 1898 inauguration, she offered the royal palace at the Hague for an international peace conference whose purpose would be the settlement of disputes by arbitration rather than force. Wilhelmina tirelessly worked to avoid the war right up to the moment it broke out, and then she contributed again to the reputation of the House of Orange as protectors of the Dutch by keeping the Netherlands out of it.

Juliana, Wilhelmina's only child, was born on April 30, 1909; the father, Prince Henry, met shortly afterward with a minister in Wilhelmina's cabinet.

"A pity," said Prince Henry, "that it is a girl."

"But, Your Royal Highness," said the cabinet minister, "I can assure you that after the nation's wonderful experience with the Dowager Queen Emma and with Queen Wilhelmina there is nobody in Holland who is not as delighted with a girl as with a boy."

"Oh, I was not doubting that," said Prince Henry. "I was thinking of the poor blighter who one day will have to be Prince Consort."

Former President Theodore Roosevelt visited Wilhelmina and Prince Henry, and Roosevelt's subsequent letter to John Hay was certainly accurate in its description of Henry, although as history would prove, it greatly underestimated Wilhelmina:

Again and again in some American country town or small city I have met a puffed-up wife of some leading grocer proud of her position . . . and resolutely insistent upon taking precedence of the other "leading ladies" of the neighborhood; well, really, Queen Wilhelmina reminded me of this type. Every other king or queen of a little country whom we encountered had good manners and refinement, and was wholly free from pretentiousness. I would not have minded poor little Wilhelmina's lacking refinement and being both common and commonplace if only she had not been pretentious. . . . Evidently she ruled her fat, heavy, dull husband with a rod of iron. He was leading a dreadful life. He told me with great pride how he had shot three elephants in Ceylon, although, unfortunately, they had no tusks; and he showed me his various hunting trophies—the ordinary hunting trophies of a German sportsman who shoots boar, deer, and roebuck in a preserve. When we got up from the lunch table the queen said to him: "Take Mr. Roosevelt into your room." He did not catch what she said, turned round with his mouth open, and asked what it was; whereupon she promptly lost her temper, grew red in the face, almost stamped her foot, and snapped out at him, "I said, *Take Mr. Roosevelt into your room,*" whereupon he gave a little start and took me into the room, in gloomy silence. Hoping to distract him, I said: "I am glad that your daughter, the little princess, seems so well." However, he declined to be diverted, and responded more gloomily than ever, and with appalling frankness: "Yes; I hope she has a brother; otherwise I pity the man that marries her!" I supposed he had been surprised into this "sad sincerity" of statement, but from something I afterwards heard I am inclined to think that it was a remark he had made on more than one occasion. I suppose he felt he had to do something, however inadequate, to salve his self-respect.

There is no question that Prince Henry was dominated by his imperious wife, but President Roosevelt was studying Queen Wilhelmina from his own unique point of view. The most macho of presidents would hardly have written kindly about a woman who looked him straight in the eye and spoke to him as an equal, or perhaps even as a *queen* to a visiting foreign citizen.

Even little Juliana could not take her father that seriously. One day she and a couple of friends were sneaking a cigarette, an offense of almost capital severity in Wilhelmina's eyes, when suddenly the door to the room was flung open. The girls froze in terror. Then Juliana relaxed when she realized it was Prince Henry. "Don't worry," she assured, "it's only Mecklenburg."

Wilhelmina had three miscarriages before Juliana was born, and it seemed, just as it had with her father, William III, that her line of the House of Orange might die out. As Alden Hatch wrote in his 1962 biography of Bernhard, "There is hardly a Dutchman over sixty who does not remember the day Princess Juliana was born. It touched off an uproarious celebration that has never been equalled in the Low Countries. Staid old gentlemen of eighty will tell you with shining eyes how drunk they got that night."

Few mothers ever loved a daughter more than Wilhelmina loved Juliana. Just seeing the two together was enough to make one recognize the strong bond between them. Wilhelmina would prove her love in many ways, never more dramatically than in the 1950s during the Greet Hofmans episode.

After the birth of Juliana, Wilhelmina devoted herself to two great tasks: keeping Holland out of the war that increasingly appeared to be inevitable, a war tiny Holland could not hope to benefit from; and managing her great personal fortune. As Alden Hatch revealed, "Unlike most kingdoms, where the royal residences belong to the state, the Queen owned several of the royal palaces personally, as well as the royal archives, the royal forests, and the other appurtenances of the monarchy." *Current Biography* would comment that Wilhelmina "has a moneyed finger in the pie of nearly every enterprise of magnitude in Holland." In fact, it was not learned until much later, and then to the chagrin of the Dutch people, that it was almost impossible to set up even a medium-sized business in the Netherlands without some sort of payment to the royal family. But that scandal involved Bernhard and did not surface for many years.

Wilhelmina's wide-ranging investments extended to the United States in 1910 when she invested $750,000 of the $2 million used to capitalize the Cullman (Alabama) Coal and Coke Company. A railroad was built, and a village for the miners, and the bulk of the coal was shipped from Mobile to the Netherlands.

Holland did manage to steer a neutral course during World War I, something for which almost everyone in the Netherlands was grateful, and still another debt was considered to be owed the House of Orange. The Dutch people were generally anti-German at the beginning of the conflict, but many became pro-German later. Germany's many investments in Holland prior to the war, including a scheme to obtain the Zuider Zee, an arm of the North Sea, made the Netherlands feel a bit of what its own colonies experienced: the economically invaded nation gained little while the outsider reaped enormous rewards.

But gradually Dutch sympathies switched to the Germans. Germany used Holland's ports during the war, and there was considerable trade between the two countries. England finally clamped on a blockade, which included confiscating almost the entire Dutch mercantile marine, and the blockade produced severe hardships. Holland's imports dropped from 4 billion guilders in 1913 to 800 million in 1917, and exports fell from 3 billion to 500 million. Also, the expense of maintaining an army on the borders was staggering, rising from 53 million guilders in 1913 to 268 million in 1916.

The Dutch suffered numerous casualties in the war,

chiefly sailors and fishermen whose ships were sunk by mines. Clothes and heating supplies were rigidly rationed, and a Food Dictator was appointed. But it was better than being occupied by one or another of the warring nations, and it certainly was preferable to freezing and dying in the stalemated trench warfare. Wilhelmina kept the Netherlands out of war, which is probably what kept her in power.

The war ended with Kaiser Wilhelm fleeing into Holland and being granted asylum; and there he remained, despite Allied demands for his extradition, a guest of Wilhelmina. Perhaps the former ruler of Germany remembered his boast about seven-foot-tall soldiers, but surely he did not repeat it to Wilhelmina.

Granting asylum to Kaiser Wilhelm, however, contributed to grave problems for Wilhelmina and her government. Monarchies were toppling at an alarming rate in Europe as the influence of Bolshevism spread, and the presence of the imperial Kaiser lent fuel to the call for revolution in the Netherlands. Dutch socialists did revolt, led by P. J. Troelstra, who called for a takeover by workers, but the monarchy was rescued by an unexpected source of support: the nation's Catholics in the southern provinces. They rallied to the Protestant Queen and put down the insurrection. One of the more dramatic scenes occurred when thousands of people gathered outside the palace at The Hague. Wilhelmina rode out into the crowd in an open carriage, and soldiers unhitched the horses and pulled the carriage themselves. Wilhelmina's appearance, with Juliana alongside, galvanized pro-monarchists throughout the nation.

But there was still a deep and underlying discontent in the Netherlands that even gratitude for the peace-keeping Queen could not long hold underground. There was a vast gulf between rich and poor, and people believed they had very little control over their own government. Only in 1917 had universal suffrage been granted to men (in 1919 for women); previously, only men of property could vote, on the theory that only those who could pay for government deserved to be represented by it. On the very night the revolution was put down, however, Wilhelmina issued a proclamation: "Social reforms shall be carried through with a speed fitting to the pulsations of our times." The proclamation itself said little enough, but it was popularly interpreted to mean that necessary social measures would be initiated. The mere fact that most people expected reforms to be carried out helped guarantee they would be.

Life in the Netherlands improved under Wilhelmina's guidance after World War I. Slum clearance programs were begun, houses and hospitals were constructed, there were wage and hour controls and old-age and unemployment insurance programs. It would all have been incomprehensible to William III; but Wilhelmina recognized the urgent need to bring Holland quickly into the twentieth century, and the country was rapidly transformed from an agricultural to an industrial nation.

Often when a new school or hospital was built, Wilhelmina appeared personally to dedicate it. This reinforced in the minds of people the image of the Queen as being associated with good works and was just one of many reasons why her popularity remained exceptionally high. Hardly anyone in the Netherlands wanted to replace the Queen.

Wilhelmina was unlike most monarchs who survived World War I in that she exercised genuine power. She possessed an absolute veto, appointed each member of the Council of State, and had the authority to dissolve the

States-General. She was consulted on everything of importance in the Netherlands, and although ministers occasionally complained that she was arrogant and abrupt, they admitted, as one observer put it, "that for statecraft, diplomacy, energy and experience the Queen is their superior." During fifty years of rule, Wilhelmina worked in harmony with more than a dozen cabinets, never once used her power of veto, and only twice dissolved the States-General.

The tiniest details of court life were spelled out by Wilhelmina and were strictly enforced by her. Light laughter was forbidden at formal receptions and frowned on at just about any other occasion. Once one of Wilhelmina's young ladies-in-waiting showed up in the latest Paris fashion.

"Where did you get that hat?" Wilhelmina asked icily.

"In Paris, Your Majesty."

"We wear Dutch clothes here," said Wilhelmina gravely.

Wilhelmina was accustomed to being obeyed. Once she boarded an American plane and waited for it to take off, but a heavy fog had descended and the pilot refused to fly until it abated. He refused to move even when Wilhelmina *ordered* him to take off. It would be different, she grumped, "if we had one of our good Dutch pilots here."

Wilhelmina was personally and politically conservative, but her reign continued to prove capable of producing startling change. There were 5 million people in the Netherlands when she assumed the throne; today there are almost 14 million and the density of population is greater than China's. If the United States had a similar population density it would contain 1.25 billion people. Under Wilhelmina vast amounts of land, formerly underwater, were reclaimed from the sea, and the Dutch fleet remained one of the finest in the world. Labor was one segment of society where her popularity was less than total: she frequently did not hesitate to call out troops to put down a strike.

Almost every morning of her life Wilhelmina prayed and studied the Bible. Her religion seemed to be genuine, not something she used to mask an acquisitive nature. Nor were her religious motives consistently base, as were those of certain other prominent Dutch. For instance, there was the banker who faithfully attended Greet Hofmans's lectures at Het Oude Looe. Finally, members of his discussion group were told they could ask Miss Hofmans the question that most concerned them about their lives. "Will I be able," the banker asked, "to cut my income tax bill next year?"

Prince Henry died in 1934, and never were there serious reports of Wilhelmina's remarrying.

When Juliana and the German Bernhard were married in 1937, Hitler hinted that it was a sign of alliance between the Netherlands and Germany. Wilhelmina vigorously and emphatically denied the suggestion. Just as she had prior to World War I, Wilhelmina worked constantly in hope of keeping Holland out of the coming conflagration.

On April 20, 1940, Hitler's fifty-first birthday and just twenty days before the invasion of the Netherlands, Wilhelmina telegraphed birthday greetings to the Führer. It was almost a pitiful attempt at urging a man who knew no mercy to show some, and in hindsight perhaps it should not have been sent. In later years the telegram would be used against Wilhelmina to try to show she had not always been hostile to the German dictator. Nevertheless, others sending telegrams included King Leopold of Belgium, King Christian of Denmark, King Carol of Romania, Prince Paul of Yugoslavia, and Regent Nicholas Horthy of Hungary.

Royal Dutch Shell was the major supplier of Germany's

oil prior to the invasion of the Netherlands on May 10, 1940. The oil, just a small percentage of which was needed in Holland, was shipped from the ports of Rotterdam and Amsterdam to Germany.

The royal family fled to England—it was a dangerous, harrowing flight—and the Netherlands, with its little "policemen's army," surrendered on May 14. As soon as Wilhelmina reached Great Britain she issued a statement explaining why she had left: to retain her freedom of action, which the Nazis certainly would have taken from her, to protect the interests of her country, and to maintain the "independence" of the Dutch East Indies. The last was self-serving, since the Dutch East Indies had no real independence, but Wilhelmina was nonetheless embarking on the heroic period of her life. Just as Winston Churchill's ringing, unforgettable words inspired the English people, no less did Wilhelmina's the Dutch. Her broadcasts on Radio Orange pulled no punches. "The archenemy of mankind, Adolf Hitler," she said in September 1941, "has tried to annihilate us. Not only has he usurped our country and bereft it of its liberty, not only have his hordes looted it and delivered our people to famine, he has also tried to rob it of its most sacred possessions by crushing its very soul. But in this he has not succeeded. On the contrary—after more than a year of suppression Holland is and feels more invincible than ever."

Nazi General Dr. Arthur Seyss-Inquart, Civil Administrator for the Netherlands, replied to Wilhelmina's broadcast:

Wilhelmina of Orange-Nassau, having learned nothing from the course of events, stubbornly adheres to the Bolshevist-capitalistic front and thereby places herself outside the commonwealth of the New Europe. She calls the . . . defense forces of the Greater German Reich the most astounding names. From the distance, and quite irresponsibly, she goads the people of Holland into a desire for sabotage and brute force against the occupying power. She incites them to actions which will only result in the harshest retaliation. At the order of the Reich's Commissioner, the Commissary-General for Public Safety has therefore stipulated that all possessions, within the occupied territory, of the living members of the House of Orange are to be confiscated. They will be devoted to purposes of public utility, in so far as they will not be requisitioned by the occupying power for the duration of the war.

"Seyss-Inquart," responded a spokesman for Wilhelmina, "pays the Queen the finest compliment an aggressor could make to the sovereign of a violated country."

Seized from Wilhelmina were two palaces at The Hague, Soestdijk Palace, a villa on the North Sea, various farms, forests, hunting estates, and other properties. The family jewels were not taken because Wilhelmina had carried them with her to England. Wilhelmina, of course, would regain all of her property, but she gained something much more important: the respect and gratitude of the Dutch people. "The government in London," said one of Holland's most courageous Resistance fighters about Wilhelmina's rule in exile, "was a bunch of chattering wives, but there was one man: the Queen."

Wilhelmina was a symbol of hope for the suffering Dutch people. They risked their lives in thousands of small acts of resistance. They wore medals bearing her picture. Gardens sprang up filled with bright orange flowers. The Nazis plowed them under. Newborn children were named for members of the House of Orange. The Nazis plowed some of the children under, too. In all, 240,000 Dutch citizens were murdered, including more than 100,000 Jews, almost every single one in the country.

Restoring war-shattered Holland was a gigantic enterprise. Some Dutch families had to make their homes in abandoned German pillboxes. People wore cardboard shoes—if they were lucky. But anything was better than the Nazis, who enforced the death penalty against people who took eggs from their own henhouse or chopped down a small tree for fuel.

When the war ended, Wilhelmina seemed to be everywhere, exhorting her subjects, praising their courage, urging them to rebuild. She seemed to be a sixty-five-year-old human dynamo. She walked through mud up to her ankles to talk with displaced persons, rode a bicycle through country towns to check on how reconstruction was proceeding.

The Marshall Plan helped, but more important was the know-how of the Dutch people and their famous industry. Food was rigidly rationed for years, three-quarters of the yearly clothing ration was needed for one suit, and a single pair of shoes was allowed each citizen every eighteen months.

Holland rebuilt. Corporate giants like Royal Dutch Shell, Philips, and Unilever were enormous even by American standards. Shell, especially, was almost a nation unto itself. But revolution in the Dutch East Indies was about to cost the Netherlands its most treasured colony, the single greatest source of its wealth, and this would be a terrific blow to the Dutch economy. Wilhelmina considered abdication.

"Slowly we approached my sixty-eighth birthday," Wilhelmina wrote in her autobiography *Lonely but Not Alone,* "which coincided with the fiftieth anniversary of my reign. Large-scale plans were being made to celebrate this jubilee. I did not feel up to this sort of thing anymore. . . ."

"In the course of the years I had seen important decisions made everywhere in the world and in many different fields. It had often struck me that the efficacy of many decisions would have been better assured if they had been made, not by people nearing the end of their lives, but by people who were still in their prime."

These were worthy thoughts, but they probably did not completely describe the pressures on Wilhelmina to abdicate. Often in history monarchs have been forced off their thrones after some catastrophic defeat, and in the eyes of Holland's upper classes the loss of the Dutch East Indies was certainly that. It spelled the end of the Netherlands as a colonial power.

On the other hand, Wilhelmina had reigned for a very long time and she felt secure in turning power over to her beloved Juliana.

Wilhelmina continued to oversee her financial empire after her abdication, but she made very few public appearances. In private she hosted people with names like Rothschild, Agnelli, and Mellon. Investment-advisers, high-powered lawyers, and accountants formed a new kind of court. There was always time for her beloved Bible.

In 1953 Wilhelmina was very visible during the disastrous floods, comforting her former subjects, a tough, compassionate old grandmother, a "rock" Juliana had called her in the inauguration address, someone who had seen everything the century so far had to offer. In 1956 Wilhelmina stepped forward to battle Bernhard and Beatrix and the others who threatened her daughter.

Mostly, though, she lived in seclusion at Het Oude Looe, praying, taking long walks, earning the reputation of a reclusive eccentric. The castle was kept cold to save on heating bills, and dark to save on electricity. Wilhelmina opened a wing of the musty old palace for disabled Resistance fighters and refugees from Indonesia and Hungary. The refugees were those who shared her conservative political beliefs.

In her last years Wilhelmina completed her autobiography. It dealt mainly with her strong religious beliefs and her faith in Christ. The book was a big seller in the Netherlands and was translated into numerous foreign languages.

Wilhelmina survived longer than almost all of her contemporaries. The Kaiser had been forced to come to her on his knees for asylum and died almost unnoticed in the Netherlands during the Second World War. The Czar of Russia had been killed. The King of Portugal was gone; so also the King of Romania and many others. The House of Orange, thanks to doughty, scrappy Wilhelmina, remained an unchanging fixture on a planet that every day seemed more willing to manage on its own without the contributions of monarchy.

Queen Wilhelmina died peacefully at the age of eighty-two on November 28, 1962, and most people in the Netherlands genuinely mourned her passing. She was honored with a "white funeral" because, in her words, it symbolized "the certainty of faith that death is the beginning of life."

4

*Even when I was a tiny girl, if I came into
a room old ladies would leap to their feet
and give me a tottering curtsy. It was so
embarrassing I almost died.*

No one was working, or even moving, when the cannons
boomed a fiftieth time. The Netherlands had come to a
stop. Here and there was a tense, whispered query—*What
is the count?*—but most people had kept careful track in
their heads. The uppermost question very soon would be
answered.

For the fifty-first time the air was shattered and the
ground shook. Buildings seemed to tremble. Although
they could have muffled their ears tight and not missed
the roar, the crowds frozen in place strained one more
time to hear the guns. But silence had descended upon
the Netherlands. The cannons would not continue to one
hundred and one and thus signify the arrival of a male.
Queen Wilhelmina and the House of Orange had given
birth to a daughter.

When Juliana was born on April 30, 1909, in the royal
palace at The Hague, two trumpeters on horseback gal-
loped through the streets proclaiming her birth. For nearly
a decade the people of Holland had prayed fervently that
Wilhelmina would give them a child, that her line of the

House of Orange would continue to govern and protect them. Now the birth of Juliana touched off nationwide celebrations. Business houses closed while people danced in the streets. People laughed and sang and drank. Even the nation's poorest citizens waited in long queues outside the royal palace to deliver their humble gifts: a scrap of clothing, some precious food, a bouquet of tulips, a priceless—for them—pair of wooden shoes.

Juliana remained in the royal palace until there was another great outpouring of affection when she was christened on June 5 at Willemskerk: Juliana Louise Emma Marie Wilhelmina, Princess of Orange-Nassau, Duchess of Mecklenburg. Each of the names had a special meaning. Juliana had been the mother of William the Silent; Louise de Coligny had been William the Silent's fourth wife; Queen Emma was Wilhelmina's mother; the Grand Duchess Marie of Mecklenburg was Juliana's paternal grandmother; and Wilhelmina herself.

Today Juliana has a long list of impressive titles. She is the Princess of Lippe-Biesterfeld; Duke of Limburg; Marquis of Veere and Flushing; Count of Katzenelnbogen, Vianden, Diez, Spiegelberg, Buren, Leerdam, and Culemborg; Burgrave of Antwerp; Baron of Breda, Diest, Beilstein, the town of Grave, the Estates of Cuyk, Ysselstein, Cranendonck, Eindhoven, Liesveld, Herstal, Warneton, Arlay, and Nozeroy; Hereditary Lord and Baron of Ameland; Lord of Borculo, Breedevoort, Lichtenvoorde, Loo, Geertruidenberg, Clundert, Zevenbergen, Upper and Lower Zwaluw, Naaldwijk, Polanen, Soest, St. Maartensdijk, Baarn, ter Fen, Willemstad, Steenbergen, Montfort, St.-Vith, Burgenbach, Daasburg, Niervaart, Turnhout, and Besançon.

"As soon as I had a moment free," Wilhelmina wrote, "I lived only for my child." It seemed to be true. Wilhelmina never seemed happier than when Juliana was on her lap. She enjoyed dressing Juliana herself, always in the finest clothes, and she would spend hours watching her play.

When Juliana was four years old the family lived in a large house in the town of Apeldoorn while Het Oude Looe was being enlarged and remodeled. Juliana played with children of the families of nobility. One game was called "Such Are Our Manners," in which Juliana would stand in the center of a circle of children and show them their manners. The game served as an early dress rehearsal for the time when Juliana would have to stand before her subjects, and Wilhelmina was delighted with the poise her daughter exhibited, "completely at ease and without any sign of shyness."

Later that same year, 1913, the royal family moved to the huge summer palace, Huis ten Bosch, just outside The Hague, which was Juliana's home for most of her childhood. Huis ten Bosch stood near the North Sea on a moat-created island accessible only by bridges. It was a magnificent place with gardens and mirror pools and "anemones and other wild flowers as far as the eye could reach." Inside the palace, everywhere Juliana looked, were rooms larger than most people's homes and paintings by the great Dutch masters. Often the family would row, by a series of picturesque lakes and canals surrounded by woods, to their lavish country estate, the Horsten.

Wilhelmina's strict and humorless court made a lasting impression on Juliana. "Even when I was a tiny girl," she remembered, "if I came into a room old ladies would leap to their feet and give me a tottering curtsy. It was so embarrassing I almost died."

Before Juliana began her formal education there were numerous lessons to be learned from her mother. At night they sat and read the Bible to each other and then quietly talked about what it meant. Wilhelmina explained to Juliana that a good earthly ruler was simply an agent of God and carried out His wishes. Wilhelmina also told Juliana about their country, only 182 miles long and 109 miles wide; about Rotterdam, soon to be the busiest port in the world; and about the mysterious, faraway colonies in the East Indies. Wilhelmina wanted nothing more than for her daughter's childhood to be different from her own: "My life had been so sheltered, allowing me only occasional glimpses of ordinary human life, that I am unable to draw a picture of the closing years of the last century. From time to time a sound penetrated through the vacuum around me; that was all."

But Wilhelmina really was not capable of allowing her daughter the personal freedom sufficient to be on intimate terms with average Dutch children, and she was mistaken if she truly believed Juliana was not shy. Most people in Holland think of their present ruler as a very shy woman.

What Wilhelmina conceived to be bold innovations designed to fight the darkness of isolation were merely slight, tentative lifts of a curtain, permitting only the narrowest shafts of light to enter. Thus, when Wilhelmina decided that Juliana should study with other youngsters her age rather than alone, a small group of carefully selected children was brought to Huis ten Bosch and educated along with Juliana by teachers from the prestigious Jan Ligthart School. In this limited atmosphere it was impossible for the children to be anything other than deferential to the young Princess, and in any case, studying with other youngsters, which began for Juliana at age six, ended when she was ten.

Although the Netherlands was a noncombatant in the First World War, some of Juliana's earliest memories were of the fighting. Distant exploding artillery could be heard at Huis ten Bosch, and on visits to Het Oude Looe Juliana could hear the battles being fought at Antwerp and Flanders. Fortunately, she was not old enough to comprehend the horrors that were all around her, nor did she understand the suffering of the flood victims of Monnikendam when she visited with her mother, but she would not long remain unaware of tragedy.

At Huis ten Bosch Juliana lived in a suite of airy rooms with a balcony facing south, and mostly she played by herself, watched closely by Wilhelmina or a governess. She loved to ride horses, catch frogs in a net, and go paddling in an old mud boat. Like every other Dutch schoolchild, she early on learned how to ride a bicycle (there are more bicycles per capita in the Netherlands than in any other nation). Juliana was an average, pleasant girl with ordinary intelligence and growing very rapidly.

Juliana completed her primary school studies, which included a course in religion taught by Wilhelmina, when she was ten, and it was not feasible for her to continue classes with other children. The Dutch Constitution stipulated that upon her eighteenth birthday she would become Queen if Wilhelmina died, and Regent if Wilhelmina was incapacitated, so a speeded-up curriculum was designed so that her secondary school studies could be behind her at that time. The subjects she was assigned closely paralleled those her mother had taken—no escaping it, there were certain topics a future monarch *had* to know—but more elbow room was allowed than Queen Emma had given Wilhelmina. Juliana learned classical languages, took lessons on the violin, and studied the history of art. Her religious education was still in the hands of her mother.

Wilhelmina continued to teach Juliana that people do

not make their own history, that "it is the will of that higher Wisdom which . . . directs the course of events through the agency of those it sends to execute the Divine Ordinance." Later, when Greet Hofmans talked about receiving messages from God, it was perhaps not surprising Juliana was willing to listen.

Juliana's first appearance as a debutante came at a dinner party on April 30, 1927, marking her eighteenth birthday. What the guests saw was a tall, rather awkward young woman who responded hesitantly to questions by expressing words of love and gratitude for her mother. Often she gazed down at her feet, then glanced quickly at Wilhelmina as though looking for approval. Juliana was perhaps the most eligible young heiress in the world, but except for a few who speculated that she would be married early because she was Wilhelmina's only hope for a continuation of her line of the House of Orange, no one was predicting an early wedding. There would be plenty of eager young suitors, gay, sophisticated nobles, but the reticent, unworldly Crown Princess was obviously not yet prepared for the responsibilities of raising a family.

Accompanied by considerable fanfare, Juliana, on September 10, 1927, entered the University of Leyden, Holland's equivalent of America's Harvard or Great Britain's Oxford, a school built by William the Silent in the town where Rembrandt was later born. Three other young women of upper-class origins went with Juliana to Leyden, where they lived in a large house in nearby Katwijk apart from the general university population. Chaperones and bodyguards followed them about, further assuring that other students would not be tempted to fraternize. Nevertheless, the four students returned home the first weekend bubbling with stories about their new adventures.

Juliana entered a class song contest her first year and the entry was judged "song of the year." It went:

> Hail our students' cell!
> Hail our girls' V.V.S.L.!
> Hail our year of heaven,
> Nineteen hundred and twenty-seven!

Wilhelmina was not impressed. "Don't get excited," she told Juliana. "They gave you the prize because you are the Princess."

When the student jury heard of Wilhelmina's skepticism, they sent her a letter assuring that the song had been selected on its merits. The Queen remained uncertain.

On another occasion, in the dressing room of Leyden's student theater, several classmates worked up their nerve and twitted Juliana about her long underwear. She was hurt by their joking and the next day ordered something more daring. When the new underclothes arrived at the royal palace, a shocked Wilhelmina sent them back.

Still another time Juliana considered wearing makeup. Wilhelmina put her foot down: "The Princess will remain as God and I made her!" Dutch wits noted that there was no mention of Prince Henry.

Juliana's college classmates remember her as shy and withdrawn, but pleasantly naive. A German diplomat suggested to her that it would be sensible if Holland and Germany were united into one country. "Oh," replied Juliana, "I think Mama is too old to rule such a large country as Germany."

There were other matters that concerned Juliana besides her progress at the University of Leyden. Upon reaching her eighteenth birthday she automatically became a member of the Council of State, and she was given her own household in the Kneuterdijk Palace at The Hague. In addition, she soon was substituting for her mother at numerous official occasions. Her first official public appearance after turning eighteen came when she and Wilhelmina visited the town of Borculo, which had been decimated by a cyclone. Many of Juliana's appearances would be at disaster sites. Much of the Netherlands is below sea level, floods are an almost daily danger, and the appearance of Juliana or Wilhelmina after a catastrophe invariably seemed to lift the spirits of the disaster victims. Nor would Juliana show up in flowing purple robes bedecked with gold, but as a concerned citizen, albeit an exalted one, dressed as a sensible Dutch woman.

At Leyden the subjects Juliana studied were chosen partly to prepare her for future duties as Queen, and partly to satisfy her interests in literature and religion. During the first year her courses included general history, pre-Napoleonic Dutch law, the customary law of the Netherlands Indies, international law, history of religion, and Dutch and French literature. Her second year was spent attending lectures on Slavic literature, mythology, Sinology, and water economy. In addition, she was tutored privately in the home of Professor C. Snouck Hurgronje on the world of Islam because it was believed she one day would rule over millions of Moslems in the East Indies.

Juliana attended the University of Leyden from September 1927 to January 1930 and was graduated with an honorary doctorate of literature and philosophy. There was a quid pro quo in this: Juliana received her doctorate, even though it was honorary, and the university could point out that the Queen had entrusted it with the education of her daughter.

"I never felt I earned it," Juliana would later say honestly about her degree. "It was a sham."

Juliana recalled overhearing one of her professors telling Prince Henry what a relaxed disposition she had.

"Ah," said Henry, "she gets that from me."

"She's very intelligent, too," the professor continued.

"That comes from her mother," said Henry.

After graduation Juliana took a skiing vacation at Oberstdorf, and the summer of 1930 was spent riding, hiking, and boating in Norway. Juliana was twenty-one and already her name was being linked to that of almost every royal bachelor in Europe. And why not? One day she would be Queen of the Netherlands, but just as important was the great fortune she would inherit, tax-free. *Time* magazine, in 1962, would declare Queen Wilhelmina to be the richest woman in the world, and of course Wilhelmina had only one child. Said *Time*: "Richest: ex-Queen Wilhelmina, Juliana's mother, whose fortune has been estimated at more than $1 billion. Queen Elizabeth's fortune, some $200 million, was founded by her shrewd great-great-grandmother Queen Victoria." In recent years, in the pecking order among royal families, it has been said that England's Queen Elizabeth blanches slightly whenever she hears the name of Juliana, one of the few women more wealthy than she.

Both Queen Emma and Prince Henry died the same year, 1934. Emma was buried next to her husband, William III, in a vault at Delft. Prince Henry was given a "white funeral," the same as Wilhelmina herself would later have.

Juliana and Wilhelmina went to Norway after Prince Henry's burial. They spent a secluded vacation, seeing only a few friends and keeping royal duties to a minimum. The proximity of death set off another round of speculation about a possible marriage partner for Juliana. Prominently mentioned were Prince Charles of Sweden, the Prince of Wales, and the brother of the Prince of Wales, the Duke of Kent. However, Juliana would end up serving as bridesmaid when the Duke of Kent married Princess Marina of Greece.

Early in 1935 Juliana accompanied her mother to the World's Fair in Brussels, and the two passed the summer vacationing in Scotland. The time had come for the eligible young Princess to marry, and much of the time was spent meeting suitors. The death of Juliana's friend Queen Astrid of Belgium in an automobile accident in Switzerland reminded Wilhelmina of the uncertainties of life. Still, Wilhelmina became more determined to supervise the courtship of Juliana and carefully screened the stampede of eager young nobles.

The 1936 Winter Olympics were held in Bavaria, and Juliana and Wilhelmina stayed at nearby Igls above Innsbruck. It was in that fairy-tale setting that Juliana met Bernhard. He drove a sports car from Paris carrying a reference from the Dutch Minister to France.

Juliana and Bernhard met again at the Olympics in Garmisch-Partenkirchen, and later he paid several secret visits to her in the Netherlands. Finally came the key meeting at Weissenburg-Bad Hotel in western Switzerland, some twenty miles from Gstaad. Juliana and Wilhelmina arrived first, and Wilhelmina was outraged to find a convention of Dutch businessmen in progress, a convention being covered by hordes of newsmen. Naturally, the Queen's unexpected arrival created a flurry of excitement. The businessmen were no problem—their convention was about to break up—but how did they shake off the reporters? Wilhelmina succeeded by granting a rare, almost unheard-of press conference in which she said she and her daughter were on a vacation and would appreciate privacy. The less-than-enterprising news corps left without what would have been a scoop.

Juliana and Bernhard were unofficially engaged during the meeting at Weissenburg-Bad, but only after hard negotiating sessions supervised by the wary Wilhelmina. Bernhard must have felt he was arranging some complicated corporate merger in which the other side held most of the assets and voting power. What Bernhard could and could not do was meticulously spelled out, as was the amount of money he could expect to receive from the state. Juliana was permitted to contribute very little to the hammering out of details. She was twenty-seven, Bernhard only twenty-five, but she really did not know much about the real world. On that subject, Bernhard knew a considerable amount.

The "Treaty of Weissenburg," as it came to be called, even mapped out how future children would be educated. Wilhelmina wanted nothing left to chance or interpretation. The "treaty" stipulated when the engagement would be made public and made Bernhard promise to quit his job with I. G. Farben in Paris and transfer to the Hollandische Koopman's Bank. Once everything was agreed upon, Bernhard returned to France. Juliana and Wilhelmina went back to the Netherlands.

The official announcement of the engagement came earlier than planned, on September 8, 1936, because it was feared the media would learn the story, and was made by Wilhelmina on nationwide radio. "I fully approve my daughter's choice," said Wilhelmina, "and consider it a wise one, seeing the excellent qualities which my future son-in-law possesses."

Juliana followed her mother on the air: "How can I describe what a happy moment it is for me to introduce my fiancé. We met during winter sports and then here again in the country and little by little we found each other and have come to an understanding. I am very, very happy."

Finally, with most of Holland listening on the radio, Bernhard: "I am anxious to learn everything there is to know about my new fatherland, the Netherlands, and I will strive to help Juliana of Orange all my life. We hope to be married in two or three months."

It seemed on the surface to be a beautiful pairing, the debonair, devoted, handsome Prince and the shy, innocent Princess. But what about beneath the surface? Was there more than met the eye? Who exactly was Prince Bernhard, and why would a good portion of the Netherlands object to the marriage?

The answers can be found in the past of Bernhard zu Lippe-Biesterfeld.

5

It would be better if the future Queen had found a consort in some democratic country rather than in the Third Reich.

LIPPE-BIESTERFELD in Western Germany has often been referred to as a "pocket principality," but in reality it was 471 square miles of land lived on by some 130,000 people. Count Ernst zu Lippe-Biesterfeld, Bernhard's grandfather, was a man powerful enough to win a jurisdictional dispute against his cousin Adolf zu Schaumburg-Lippe, who was married to the very important Princess Victoria of Hohenzollern, Kaiser Wilhelm's sister. At stake was nothing less than control of Lippe-Biesterfeld, and the fact that Bernhard's grandfather emerged victorious said a great deal about the influence he wielded in autocratic Germany.

Bernhard's father, also Prince Bernhard, married Baroness Armgard von Sierstorpff-Cramm, and on June 29, 1911, the future Prince of the Netherlands was born in Jena. He was christened Bernhard Leopold Friedrich Eberhard Julius Kurt Karl Gottfried Peter zu Lippe-Biesterfeld. Bernhard's brother, Aschwin, whose later alleged ties to the Nazis would prove embarrassing, was born in 1914.

The elder Prince Bernhard, a Prince Major in the Kaiser's army, served on the Western Front and was awarded two Iron Crosses and the Bavarian Order of the Crossed Swords. He returned to his family in 1917, his hair having turned white from the carnage he had witnessed, in the hope of salvaging his principality. It was not to be, although he was more fortunate than his brother, Prince Leopold zu Lippe, who was literally dragged from his castle by a throng of angry peasants. There were also plenty of disillusioned soldiers and peasants trying to murder the elder Prince Bernhard—one soldier took a shot at him—but he escaped with his life and a considerable fortune, although he did lose the principality.

One of Bernhard's more colorful earlier ancestors was a saint, Saint Bernhard, whom the future Prince of the Netherlands described as "quite a bad fellow. Devoted most of his life to pillage and such. Later, he made amends by bringing Christianity to the people of the Baltic, and some Pope made him a saint, which I don't think he deserved."

Juliana's future husband was tutored at his new home in Reckenwalde until he was twelve and then attended a boarding high school at Zuellichau in what is now East Germany. Bernhard was constantly being beaten up by classmates who resented his being a Prince. One young man in particular chose every Sunday afternoon to flail him with a belt buckle. Finally, home for a short vacation, Bernhard confessed that he did not want to return to school. His mother, the feisty, pipe-smoking Baroness Armgard, had a different solution: "Kick him in the stomach," she advised.

Young Bernhard was confirmed in the Lutheran Church when he was fourteen, and he remembers the advice his father gave him: "Beware of vanity, haughtiness, and self-conceit; be honest, respect women; meet everybody openly and honestly and show even the least of people a friendly face. Before all, exercise self-discipline, for only this makes a man a true Christian.

"You have two of the most precious gifts of God, my child; your golden heart and your good brain. . . . use your heart and brain in the right way and you won't miss the straight road. . . . I will say everything again in these words: 'Become a knightly German and a Christian.'"

After three years at Zuellichau, Bernhard transferred to a boarding high school in Berlin. It was a school whose dormitories were named for ruling families. Bernhard lived in Orange House.

Bernhard went on to study law at the University of Lausanne in Switzerland and at the universities of Munich and Berlin. By all accounts, including his own, he was not a particularly serious student at the first two schools, preferring drink and the company of beautiful women to the pursuit of book learning. But at the University of Berlin something suddenly happened. "In one year," as his admiring biographer Alden Hatch pointed out, "he completed the law course for the *Referendaris-Juris,* the legal equivalent of a Ph.D., and passed the final examination, which three out of four candidates fail on their first attempt."

The University of Berlin was a hotbed of Nazi activity during 1934, Bernhard's last year of study. The sons of nobles whose fathers had lost their land were among the most avid supporters of Hitler, and these were precisely the people who crowded the halls of Berlin University in 1934. They were Bernhard's friends. One was a man named Langenheim, who later would use Bernhard for Nazi Intelligence purposes. After this occurred, Bernhard would argue passionately and convincingly that he had been unwittingly taken advantage of by a former friend.

While in his final year at the University of Berlin, Bernhard joined the League for Air Sports, an outfit posing as a sports club but one that actually was training Hitler's future war pilots. Bernhard said he quit the League for Air Sports before he could be cashiered after he and a friend crashed a plane into a lake. Nevertheless, just as his previously lackluster academic career had suddenly blossomed, he just as suddenly joined the motorized SS, those black-shirted bullies whose brutal terror tactics would become abhorred by the entire civilized world. Bernhard said later his stint in the SS was harmless, that he joined because it made it easier for him to finish his law studies and because he enjoyed participating in "what almost amounted to a sports car rally."

Bernhard explains that he resigned from the SS upon receiving his law degree. But did he? And if he did, what role did he assume next?

Bernhard went to work in Paris for I. G. Farben, the mammoth German chemical conglomerate that, among many other things, was busy stockpiling war matériel for the Third Reich. I. G. Farben later manufactured the gas that was used at Auschwitz. But as to Bernhard's role, *Newsweek* revealed much later, April 5, 1976: "According to testimony at the Nuremberg trials after World War II, Bernhard before the war was a contact man in an industrial-espionage network that Farben was running for the German government."

The League for Air Sports. The SS. Industrial spying for I. G. Farben. Had the Dutch people been apprised of all of Bernhard's activities, his upcoming marriage to Juliana probably would have been opposed even more vigorously. As it was, most opposition, except that of an acutely political nature, came from those who remembered another German, the late, extremely unpopular Prince Henry.

Another member of the industrial-espionage network to which Bernhard belonged was Gunther Frank-Fahle, who would show up in West Germany after the war as an agent of Lockheed. Frank-Fahle's good right arm would be a man named Ernest Hauser, and both would figure in the bribery scandals that crashed down on Bernhard in the 1970s.

The September 8, 1936, announcement of Juliana's engagement to Bernhard contributed to the polarization of a sizable portion of the Netherlands. Jewish citizens were particularly outraged. Already there was an active, vocal Dutch Nazi Party in Holland, but now party members openly paraded with swastikas. There was brawling in the streets of Amsterdam between Nazis and anti-Nazis. Swastikas were painted on walls and buildings and were as quickly removed. Tensions were not cooled when former Kaiser Wilhelm, living at Doorn, sent a letter of congratulations to Wilhelmina, and when Adolf Hitler forwarded his own congratulatory message. The newspaper *Het Volk* editorialized that "it would be better if the future Queen had found a consort in some democratic country rather than in the Third Reich."

Wilhelmina repeatedly assured her subjects that no alliance of any sort should be inferred from the Juliana-Bernhard marriage. Wilhelmina simply wished the fuss would go away. She realized it was of paramount importance for Juliana to marry quickly, that without a grandchild her family would become legally extinct, and she could not forget her own three miscarriages. The States-General could, of course, invite foreign royalty to reign over Holland's constitutional monarchy, but that was unlikely. Dutch citizens were loyal to the House of Orange, not monarchy per se. Also, that solution did not appeal in the least to Wilhelmina and her strong sense of the House of Orange's personal destiny. Having waited so long to see Juliana marry, she now was in a hurry to see the fruits.

Baroness Armgard, Bernhard's mother (his father, like Juliana's, had died in 1934), also would soon find herself caught up in political intrigue. She was from the same family that produced the great German tennis player von Cramm, most famous perhaps for losing, after a personal telephone call from Adolf Hitler, the most important match of his career, in the U.S. championship, to Don Budge. When Baroness Armgard hoisted the flag of the House of Orange over her German home, she was visited by the local SS commander who insisted she fly the swastika alongside. Her compliance created more controversy in the Netherlands.

Shortly before the wedding Bernhard met Adolf Hitler in the Reich Chancellery. The purpose of the meeting was to request permission from the Führer to give up his rights as a German citizen. Hitler's remembrance of that meeting and his recollections of Prince Henry have a ring of sad authenticity, even though it should be remembered that the speaker was one of history's consummate liars: "In Holland, thank goodness, things are much easier, for in Prince von Lippe-Biesterfeld we have an absolute imbecile oaf on the throne. When, before his marriage, he came to pay me a farewell visit, he cringed and scraped like a gigolo. A couple of days later, he declared in the Dutch press that in his heart he had always felt himself a Dutchman.

"The late Prince Consort of Queen Wilhelmina was also a typical royal idiot. He even had the impertinence to approach me, shortly after our assumption of power, for a loan of seven and a half million guilders, in return for his assurance that he would then do all in his power to increase German influence in Holland."

Newspapers in Germany criticized preparations for the upcoming marriage. The *Essner National Zeitung,* considered the personal voice of Hermann Göring, reminded Bernhard that he was first a German and should use his influence to put a halt to what the newspaper viewed as unpleasant and insulting incidents. These included "demonstrations" by "certain elements" in the Netherlands against display of the swastika flag and the failure of Dutch police to deal harshly with the protesters. Other National Socialist newspapers complained that at official functions attended by Juliana and Bernhard the playing of the Dutch national anthem was not followed by "Deutschland Über Alles" or the "Horst Wessel Lied," the joint national anthems of Nazi Germany.

Bernhard was granted Dutch citizenship by royal order on November 24, 1936, and was thereby obliged to change the spelling of his names from German to Dutch. Peter was altered to Pieter, Kurt to Coert, and so on. Bernhard was extremely busy in the months before his marriage, dividing his time between attending official receptions and studying the colonial situation in the East Indies. He also worked to improve his halting Dutch.

On Christmas Eve, 1936, Juliana and Bernhard complied with the law by registering their intention to marry, and the notice was affixed to the doors of the Stadhuis in The Hague. What ensued was known as "The Bride's Days," a happy period of balls, receptions, and parties that scandalized members of Wilhelmina's court but were in reality quite tame and proper. Juliana herself was glowing, quite obviously a young woman happily in love. She had never been permitted to meet anyone remotely resembling the dapper Bernhard, and the life that stretched before her seemed bright indeed. She called her fiancé Bernilo, she was Jula, and even in the intellectual sphere there appeared unlimited new vistas. Just before the wedding Juliana and Bernhard took part in a series of discussions with Dutch citizens holding a variety of views, even Communist. The discussions were to dispel the notion that Bernhard was somehow undemocratic, but they were fascinating for Juliana, whose previous experiences had revolved around obsequious footmen, saluting aides, foot-clicking coachmen, servile couriers, curtsying ladies-in-waiting, and bowing, favor-seeking burgomasters. Some of those in the discussion groups did not mince words, and perhaps for the first time Juliana learned that the House of Orange was not universally loved.

Problems persisted right up almost to the moment of the wedding. Three German princesses scheduled to be bridesmaids had their passports confiscated by the SS, and only Wilhelmina's intervention enabled two of them to get across the border. They arrived with only 10 marks each ($4.02), but Wilhelmina provided extra pocket money. In fact, she seemed to be providing everything, including twelve sets of long underwear, one for each of the bridesmaids: the two German princesses, who were cousins of Bernhard, a Dutch girl to substitute for the missing princess, the three young women who had gone off to the University of Leyden with Juliana, and six members of the Dutch nobility.

Bernhard was declared Prince of the Netherlands on the day before his marriage. After the wedding he would begin drawing 200,000 florins ($109,500) a year from the state. Prince Henry had never been allowed any income from the government, which might partially explain why he tried to negotiate a deal with Adolf Hitler.

On the eve of the wedding there was a giant reception at The Hague. Holland's nobility, rich businessmen, and guests from numerous countries of the world gathered amid breathtaking surroundings to meet the next Queen of the Netherlands. Juliana, Wilhelmina, and Bernhard, along with Wilhelmina's large court and Juliana's smaller one, sat at one end of the huge hall. The foremost question in everyone's mind was whether "Deutschland Über Alles" and the "Horst Wessel Lied" would be played. They were, but by a military band. Twenty-five musicians in the regular band, supported by their conductor, refused to play the Nazi anthems. Also scheduled for the guests was a group of Dutch comedians, the chief one of whom would appear on stage as Kaiser Wilhelm and gradually strip out of his finery until he was the living image of Adolf Hitler. This act was scratched and some nonpolitical British comedians took its place. Even powerful Wilhelmina did not feel she could risk the ire of the German Führer.

Hitler was only partially mollified. Orders were given to Prince Friedrich zu Wied, an avid Nazi and one of Bernhard's groomsmen, not to attend the reception at The Hague. Wilhelmina appointed in his place Professor Jan Huizinga, an anti-Nazi teacher and writer who once had taught Juliana history. Every German correspondent who had come to report on the wedding, except one, acted on prior instructions from Propaganda Minister Goebbels and walked out. The correspondent who stayed also acted under orders from Goebbels.

It was Juliana's marriage, but Wilhelmina was in charge. A cabinet minister told her there were 180 newsmen who wanted seats inside the church. "Do you not think four would be enough?" countered the Queen. Eventually, 108 got in.

Thousands of Dutch citizens contributed money to buy

Juliana a yacht as a wedding present. It was to be a magnificent seagoing vessel. After the money was collected, Wilhelmina stepped in and decided it would be spent on a Dutch canal yacht and for remodeling Soestdijk Palace.

Finally the wedding was at hand. One of the only two offspring produced by the House of Orange in eighty years was about to be married. It promised to be one of the great social events of the century.

6

We do not sue our people.

OUTSIDE THE fifteenth-century Groote Kerk—the Church of St. James—stood sixty of Juliana's college classmates; nearby at rigid attention were two lines of grim-faced cadets from the Dutch East Indies; in front of these a single line of Royal Navy cadets; surrounding the Great Church, "100,000 Dutch girls," brightly clad peasant children wearing gold in their bonnets, the accumulated savings of many lifetimes; at the actual entrance of Groote Kerk, and across the street at that of City Hall, fifteen hundred ramrod-straight, clear-eyed, apple-cheeked young officers born in the same year as either Juliana or Bernhard; throughout the city, ten thousand soldiers; and everywhere, more than one million people, clogging the streets, crushed up against one another, many dressed in orange, hoping, despite the tremendous odds, for a glimpse of the Crown Princess.

She rode in a gold coach pulled by eight coal-black horses. The nature of her bridal gown, much speculated about, was concealed by a stunning ermine cape. Next to her was Bernhard, dressed in the glittering black uniform of the Blue Hussars, with blue braids and red military sash. He looked taller than his five feet nine inches, much taller than Juliana, who was only an inch shorter. It was a deliberately prepared illusion, as would be so many photographs of the royal couple in the future.

Troops preceded the golden carriage—otherwise it could not have moved—pushing gently forward through the overcast morning. The glittering little parade was completed by two smaller coaches carrying Queen Wilhelmina, her brother-in-law the Duke of Mecklenburg, the sporty Baroness Armgard, and Bernhard's brother, Aschwin. Continuous cheering welled up from each side and rumbled up ahead as the procession came into view.

They stopped first at City Hall to sign the register and be united in civil marriage by the Burgomaster of The Hague. People gasped when they saw for the first time how Juliana was dressed: in a heavy gown of ivory satin with a train eighteen feet long, a tulle veil embroidered with silver and topped by a crown of orange blossoms; the incredible gown had a high neck with long sleeves, and the veil was held in place by five silver roses.

The Burgomaster of The Hague launched into the Dutch uncle lecture that all married people in the Netherlands hear. He said that marriage was difficult, trying, that wealth is the result of industry, responsibility comes before pleasure, joy is tempered by sorrow, that integrity and honesty go hand in hand with power. Wilhelmina shuffled her feet. Would the man never stop? She had set up a timetable and the Burgomaster was tearing it to shreds.

Across the street in Groote Kerk a representative of England's Queen Mary, the Duke of Kent, was fuming. He did not appreciate being kept waiting, it was made abundantly clear. Contributing to his impatience might have been the knowledge that he often had been mentioned, before his marriage to Princess Marina, as a possible husband for Juliana. A Dutch cabinet minister offered the Duke of Kent some chocolate but it was waved away. The English did not eat in church.

The Burgomaster was still lecturing. He mentioned humility, charity, thrift, compassion, generosity, and understanding. Juliana wore a serene, contented smile. Wilhelmina was boiling mad.

At last they headed across the street for the religious ceremony, and sixteen hundred notables craned their necks to watch Juliana walk down the long aisle of Groote Kerk, her train carried by four children, the twelve bridesmaids arrayed behind her in six pairs and dressed in varying pastels to produce a rainbow effect. Juliana stumbled once, just as she was about to sit in one of the bridal chairs, and moments later a diamond bracelet bearing seventeen hundred stones fell from her arm and was retrieved by Bernhard.

Bernhard promised that he would "never leave her and will love and faithfully keep her as a true and godly man should keep his lawful wife" and to "live in harmony with her, swearing to be faithful and true in all things as taught by Holy Scripture."

Juliana promised to "obey, serve and help him, never leave him, live in harmony and remain true to him and act in all things as a godly and faithful wife is bound to act toward her husband as taught by Holy Scripture."

Bernhard was then asked if he would "take this woman . . ."

"*Ja!*" he boomed, his voice resounding in the church and startling many of the guests.

Only a few guests standing nearby heard Juliana's faint response when asked if she would "take this man . . ."

The return to the royal palace for the wedding breakfast touched off wild cheering along the procession's route. The normally reserved Dutch people let themselves go in a spontaneous display of joy and affection that brought tears to the eyes of the Crown Princess. The sun even burst through as the coaches wound their way through the streets of The Hague.

Another wedding took place in the Netherlands on January 7, 1937. A special law had been passed forbidding marriages on this day, but a plea to Wilhelmina permitted a single exception. The bride, who became known as "The Other Juliana," was a poor peasant woman named Petronella van der Meer from the village of Oegstgeest, and she was marrying a seller of vegetables named Martinus van Stijn. Petronella van der Meer had been born on the same day and at approximately the same time as Juliana, which was why the exception was granted. Reporters from many parts of the world traveled to Oegstgeest to cover the wedding of "The Other Juliana," and they heard the Dutch uncle lecture delivered by the Vice-Burgomaster who performed the ceremony: "You two young people must not get the idea that you are of any importance because all these people have come here while you are married. Your marriage would not have been noticed had it not been celebrated on the same day as that of the Crown Princess. You are not of the least importance. I offer my congratulations and good wishes."

Juliana's marriage was broadcast live in the United States over radio stations WEAF, WABC, and WJZ. In New York, formerly New Amsterdam, more than one hundred persons of Dutch-American ancestry went across the Hudson River to New Jersey to celebrate aboard the Holland-America liner *Statendam*.

A special train was waiting to carry Juliana and Bernhard to Igls, near Innsbruck, where Bernhard had driven to meet his future bride, for the royal honeymoon. The two left the wedding breakfast after only an hour and ostensibly boarded the train, which then steamed to Igls and a gala welcome. When the train arrived the entire village was on hand, including the town councilmen and the local band, which struck up the Dutch national anthem. But Juliana and Bernhard were not aboard the train; it had been employed as a ruse to throw off reporters. The royal couple had returned to the palace by a side entrance and danced and sang at a party until 5 A.M. In charge of this deception was Premier Hendricus Colijn, often described as "stuffy" and "imperious" where politics were concerned, but his hoax worked so well that Wilhelmina awarded him the highest honor the House of Orange could confer, the Grand Cross of the Order of the Netherlands Lion.

Juliana and Bernhard honeymooned in Krynica, the magnificent ski resort in the Carpathian Mountains of southern Poland. When newsmen caught up with them two days later, they found a cheerful, beaming Juliana falling down on a practice slope while the devil-may-care Bernhard was zipping down steep mountain inclines. Juliana learned only two words in Polish: "Don't photograph!"

The honeymooning couple was accompanied by Captain Sesink, Wilhelmina's chief security officer, a husky, powerful, deep-chested young man "who looked exactly like an American detective." Sesink adopted a protective attitude toward the royal couple where journalists were concerned, but the zealous, burly bodyguard made Bernhard edgy. Nothing could be done about him, however.

Juliana was having the time of her life. It was her first taste of real freedom, and she even smoked cigarettes and drank whiskey and soda in public. Wilhelmina, who was vacationing at Igls to soothe local feelings about her daughter's not showing up, made her displeasure clear in private communications to Juliana. It was not long before Wilhelmina's unhappiness—which she blamed on Bernhard, for leading her daughter astray—flared into public headlines.

Juliana's honeymoon lasted for months. She and Bernhard visited the Tyrol, Budapest, Rome, Monte Carlo, and Vienna, accompanied always by the dour Captain Sesink. Once they tried to lose Wilhelmina's eagle eye by speeding away from him in a fast car. They took a circuitous route, darting through side streets and down back alleys. Later, at their destination in front of the famous Monte Carlo Casino, a friend pulled out a pistol and fired a blank. "I wonder what Sesink's face would look like if he had heard that," said Bernhard.

Sesink popped out from behind some bushes. "Just as it always does, Your Royal Highness," he said.

After the honeymoon finally ended in Paris, Juliana and Bernhard moved into the remodeled Soestdijk Palace near Utrecht in the heart of the Netherlands. Although Juliana would later own Soestdijk, for the time being Wilhelmina was charging rent and this was a source of endless irritation to Bernhard. He even complained to journalists, which irritated Wilhelmina.

Soestdijk Palace is a very long, low white building constructed in a semicircle and surrounded by a park. It was built in the seventeenth century, enlarged by Louis Bonaparte, and continually added to and improved in years that followed. Soestdijk Palace contained more than a hundred fabulous, treasure-filled rooms, but was never used for large official receptions. These were held at the royal palace in Amsterdam, which contains the largest hall in Europe.

There were tens of thousands of wedding presents for Juliana to check over when she returned from her honeymoon. They ranged from valuable jewelry and expensive automobiles to humble homemade clothes left by devoted peasants. Their sheer numbers dramatically demonstrated the popularity of the House of Orange in the Netherlands.

Juliana, looking radiant, was accorded a tumultuous welcome on her first official visit to Amsterdam. Several days later, June 15, 1937, she went on nationwide radio to thank people for the reception and to announce that she was expecting a child. It was no wonder that journalists wrote about the "Idyll of Soestdijk."

Early on the morning of November 29, 1937, near Amsterdam, the car Bernhard was driving at almost one hundred miles per hour collided with a truck. The car, said Bernhard, was "a supercharged Ford that went like a bomb." Bernhard was taken to the hospital, unconscious and with a broken neck and ribs, and Wilhelmina at Het Oude Looe was the first to be notified. The doctors were fearful for Bernhard's life, and Wilhelmina had to break the news to Juliana as delicately as possible. Juliana, seven months pregnant, moved into a hospital room adjoining Bernhard's, and he surprised everyone, including his doctors, by making a rapid recovery. Juliana's love for Bernhard seemed strengthened by his accident, but subsequent "episodes" would strain the marriage almost to the breaking point.

When Bernhard was conscious and alert, he suggested filing a lawsuit for damages against the truck driver with whom he'd had the accident. Despite Bernhard's high rate of speed, there was evidence that the other driver might be at fault. Visions of a member of the superwealthy House of Orange suing a truck driver—and the inevitable bad publicity—chilled Wilhelmina's heart. "We do not sue our people," she told Bernhard frostily.

* * *

Princess Beatrix, nicknamed Trix, arrived on January 31, 1938, and the cannons boomed fifty-one times to tell the people of the Netherlands that a female heir to the throne had been born. There was plenty of late-night revelry, as when Juliana was born, but not the all-out celebrations that greeted Wilhelmina's only child. It was expected Juliana would have more children, and of course she had not gone through three miscarriages as her mother had. Beatrix was next in line after Juliana unless a son was born, in which case he would take precedence.

Souvenir and trinket manufacturers in the Netherlands, anticipating Juliana's first child, produced large quantities of knickknacks dated "January 1938" to commemorate the expected birth. When Beatrix finally was born, on the last day of the month, she and her mother were credited with saving the manufacturers from financial losses. It was a good start for the Crown Princess and her daughter in business-conscious Holland.

The new Princess was christened Beatrix Wilhelmina Armgard at St. Jacobskerk in The Hague. The royal family rode to the christening in the great golden coach, and again there were cheering throngs of well-wishers, although nothing approaching the masses who had turned out for the wedding. *Beatrix* meant "she who brings happiness," and the name was apt for the Netherlands of 1938, which yearned for a continuation of rule by the House of Orange: war was in the offing, and people prayed the reigning family could once again keep Holland out of it.

The godfather of Beatrix was King Leopold of Belgium and the godmothers were Princess Alice, Queen Emma's sister, and Countess Kotzebue, Bernhard's aunt. When the priest sprinkled water over Beatrix's head, her cries filled the church and went into tens of thousands of Dutch homes that were following the ceremony on nationwide radio.

It was just before the christening that Wilhelmina and Bernhard had their first public run-in. They had been quarreling privately, almost since the outset of the marriage, about smoking and drinking in public and Bernhard's penchant for boating or skiing on Sunday, which Wilhelmina believed should be set aside for prayer. But when Bernhard proposed that he and Juliana go on a cruise in April 1938, Wilhelmina had heard enough. She said that Beatrix was too young to be without her mother and told Juliana she should not go. Juliana stayed home, reluctantly, but as time passed she became less hesitant about listening to her mother. In later years she would increasingly and rightly be compared to Wilhelmina, particularly in areas involving her husband.

Juliana's trademark had always been the immaculate white gloves she wore, just as Bernhard's was a fresh white carnation tucked jauntily in his lapel, and the gloves might have told something about Juliana as a mother. Beatrix's nurse related how if a rattle or toy even came in contact with the floor, it had to be sterilized immediately. The nurse was also amused by the way Beatrix was fed: a footman would arrive carrying a huge silver tray with a domed cover; inside were "a few spoonfuls of hot strained oatmeal."

Additional information began to surface about Bernhard that had to alarm Dutch security forces, concerned as they were about the possibility of a German invasion. It was learned that just before Bernhard's marriage to Juliana he had invited a man named Langenheim, an outspoken Nazi and a member of the SS unit to which Bernhard had belonged, to stay several days at Het Oude Looe, where he and Juliana were living. Bernhard talked to Langenheim openly about the internal situation in the Netherlands and offered his personal assessment of the Dutch Nazi Party. Langenheim thereupon promptly relayed the entire conversation to Foreign Minister Joachim von Ribbentrop. Also disturbing to the Dutch and embarrassing to Bernhard was the fact that his brother, Aschwin, had professed loyalty to the Nazis when he was sixteen years of age in 1930, something he would later apologize for and admit was a mistake. Talking to Langenheim, as Bernhard did, and supporting the Nazis at age sixteen, as Aschwin had, might not seem like important occurrences in normal times, but the Netherlands in the late 1930s was not passing through a normal period.

The gathering clouds in Europe cast a shadow over what should have been extremely happy days for Juliana. But the question, as she well knew, was not whether Hitler would attack the Netherlands, but when. Juliana took pride in supervising all housework at Soestdijk Palace, helping to prepare menus, and keeping a close eye on the precious Beatrix. "Do not laugh at these fat legs," she once joked. "Upon them stand the hopes of the House of Orange." Now there was a second pair of legs to carry those hopes.

And soon there was another. On August 5, 1939, the people of the Netherlands listened still again as the cannons roared fifty-one times. The little girl, like Beatrix born in Soestdijk Palace, was named Irene Emma Elizabeth: Irene for the much-hoped-for peace; Emma for her great-grandmother; and Elizabeth for the Queen of England, who was her godmother. The honorary godfathers were every soldier in Holland.

Beatrix was only nineteen months old at the time of Irene's birth, but already, aided by a governess, she was allowed to wade in the family's 150-foot swimming pool. Beatrix by this time had developed a distinct personality and there were disagreements between Juliana and Bernhard on how she should be disciplined. Once Beatrix threw a plate of vegetables on the carpet and Bernhard wanted to spank her. "No, no," said Juliana. "Chastisement does not convince. Scolding is quite enough." Later, however, when Bernhard became convinced that Beatrix had purposely wet her pants, he did administer the spanking.

These really should have been the happiest times for Juliana, the young, rich wife and mother with an entire nation prepared to do her bidding. But history was about to intervene, and life was going to change for Juliana, mostly for the worse.

7

*And then there are my two children. You
will see them among you. Indeed you will see
them quite often for we do not like to lock
ourselves up. It is just not in our nature. I
hope you will be kind to them. I am their
mother and therefore I rather think they are
very sweet children. Above all things they
smile quite easily. Please give them your smile
and they will be happy and they will ask for
very little more. That I think is about all
there is to tell.*

THE GERMAN ARMIES smashed into the Netherlands on
May 10, 1940, and the undermanned, poorly equipped
Dutch fought back bravely. Reich planes destroyed the
cities, Nazi troops prowled the countryside, and the help-
less people could do little but look on in terror. But many
Dutch were still fighting when they were stunned a
second time.

Over the radio came the news that the royal family and
the government had fled to England. People listened in
disbelief; in fact, they at first *refused* to believe. But it
was true, and it seemed to many that they had been
abandoned in their moment of greatest need. The Germans, and their friends the Dutch Nazis, were quick to
assure that such was precisely the case; yet the nation

where Anne Frank would write, a nation whose territory had not been invaded since the days of Napoleon, fought on until to continue would have been suicide. There were five bloody, nightmarish days, a lifetime, before the Netherlands capitulated—but in spirit she never gave up.

Juliana, Bernhard, Beatrix, and Irene escaped in an armored truck owned by the Bank of the Netherlands. The truck was fronted by a car full of soldiers and trailed by a vehicle carrying the redoubtable Captain Sesink and several of his men. Irene slept on Juliana's lap, Beatrix sat with a nurse, Bernhard cradled a machine gun under his arm—a machine gun with which he had tried to knock down a plane earlier—and on the floor of the armored car, in a cardboard box, were the crown jewels of the Netherlands. It took four hours to negotiate the forty miles from The Hague to Ijmuiden on the North Sea, where the H.M.S. *Codrington* was waiting to take them to relative safety in England.

"We won't be back for five years at least," said Captain Sesink when they were aboard the ship.

"Five years!" scoffed Bernhard. "What nonsense!"

Wilhelmina and the Dutch government left the next day. They too took a British ship that landed them at Harwich, and Wilhelmina would recall that Juliana and Bernhard "were very upset and did not understand why I had to follow them so soon." Later the Dutch people would be split on the issue. Some believed Wilhelmina should have remained and shared the fate of her countrymen, especially since her succession was assured by Juliana and the girls in England. Others argued that her presence would have served no purpose and that she was right in seizing the opportunity to escape. Almost all agree that she was a tower of strength in Great Britain.

Wilhelmina was not the only head of a government-in-exile in England, but none performed as well as she. Also in London were King Haakon of Norway, Grand Duchess Charlotte of Luxembourg, the ministers of Poland and Belgium, General Charles de Gaulle of Free France, and President Beneš of Czechoslovakia. They would be joined in 1941 by King Constantine of Greece and King Peter of Yugoslavia.

The Germans, after their initial propaganda success in exploiting Wilhelmina's departure, were sorry the Queen had left. Her frequent broadcasts on Radio Orange, usually at night, were eagerly awaited by almost everyone in the Netherlands. Most listened huddled in basements, knowing that to be caught meant arrest, concentration camp, possibly death.

Bernhard returned to Zeeland as soon as Juliana was settled, a courageous action, but he could do nothing more than join the Dutch forces in their retreat. He went on to Paris for an interview with Marshal Pétain, then returned to England in a patrol boat. Later the Dutch press would portray Bernhard as a war hero, and his broadcasts to the underground Resistance did boost morale, but his exploits as "The Fighting Prince" were exaggerated. He became more a behind-the-lines commander-in-chief of Holland's Resistance fighters, which does not take away from his actual contributions to the war effort.

Juliana and the children were living in a house in Gloucestershire loaned to them by Lord Bledisloe. The decision had already been made that they would have to leave England for Canada. There was the very real danger of a German invasion of Great Britain, and it would not do for the entire House of Orange to be captured or killed. This was of such genuine concern that Juliana, Wilhelmina, and the children never traveled on the same airplane out of fear that they all might perish at once. They did not want even to stay in the same house in Great Britain.

King George loaned two huge Daimlers to the Dutch royal family and on June 2, 1940, they drove to Cardiff in Wales where the Dutch ship *Sumatra* was docked. Including Juliana, the royal entourage consisted of eleven people: Juliana's aide-de-camp and his wife, a governess, a cook, and a team of security men headed by the recently promoted Colonel Sesink. One of the security men was carrying the crown jewels.

Beatrix was sick when the royal party boarded the *Sumatra*. She had German measles, which Juliana had not allowed to be treated by an English doctor, preferring to wait until they were aboard the *Sumatra* and could see a Dutch physician.

The voyage to Canada was fun for the children but harrowing for their mother. Dutch sailors, among the best in the world at *sailing,* fed the ten-month-old Irene brown beans, bacon, hunks of pork, and thick pea soup. The sailors also gave her chocolate sauce and ice cream. One day Beatrix was caught drinking a bottle of gin. She had thought it was lemonade and roared when it was taken away from her. The sailors, for their part, thought the children were delightful.

Juliana stayed in the first officer's cabin, rejecting the captain's offer of his own quarters. She and everyone aboard except the child princesses were tense and fearful throughout the voyage. The cruiser *Sumatra* was accompanied by a submarine-hunting destroyer, and on the third day there was an alarm. It came to nothing, but Juliana was sobered as she watched preparations to launch the lifeboats. On another occasion the destroyer was away for three days. That this was wartime was further driven home by the order that no smoking was allowed on deck, and by the realization that the Germans would love to sink the ship carrying the Crown Princess of the Netherlands and thus end the reign of the House of Orange.

When they were at last docked at Halifax, Juliana spoke to the crew of the *Sumatra*. She thanked them for herself and her daughters as tears brimmed in her eyes. She said she understood their loneliness and gave concern for their families back in the Netherlands suffering under the Nazi boot. Then she went ashore and the *Sumatra* sailed for the Dutch East Indies. More than half the crew was dead before the war ended.

Back in England Wilhelmina was all business. She had issued a statement to the Dutch people only hours after her arrival in Great Britain, and then she immediately set about establishing a chain of command and her authority over the Dutch government officials in exile. No one doubted for a moment that Wilhelmina was in charge. Her ancestors William III and William IV would have understood: they too had taken command when it appeared the nation might vanish from the map.

In private Wilhelmina spoke of being able to carry on the war for as long as ten years, so rich were she, other private Dutch citizens, and the government itself. Long before the Germans had attacked the Netherlands, gold and other assets had been transferred out of the country and centralized for safety. And soon Wilhelmina found herself richer still. As the Japanese moved to take over the Dutch East Indies, the value of Royal Dutch Shell stock began to skyrocket. It seemed an inexplicable phenomenon, but in reality it made good sense. Private German investors, many of them the original financial muscle behind Hitler, were driving up the price of the stock in anticipation of the Japanese controlling the East Indies. But Wilhelmina was not outsmarted. She and other Dutch investors threw in their own money to buy even more Royal Dutch Shell stock and to push the price even beyond the means of the Germans.

Wilhelmina moved away from her bomb-endangered home near Victoria Station to a house in Stubbings, about an hour by car from London. A special guard of armed soldiers protected her around the clock. Wilhelmina attended Protestant religious services regularly and insisted that her staff go also.

In the Netherlands itself there were heroes and knaves, but most people, most of the time, adopted an attitude of sullen acceptance. They despised the German occupiers, and they would rise up when there was a chance of victory, but they wanted to survive. One of the knaves was Hendricus Colijn, the Premier who had arranged the train subterfuge at the time of Juliana's honeymoon. Colijn met with Arthur Seyss-Inquart and said he was willing to cooperate with the Nazis. Later he claimed Hitler was justified in his aggression because of the unfair Treaty of Versailles, and he became fond of speaking out against "the evils of democracy," which he listed as an excessive reliance on the desire of voters and the unwarranted tendency of citizens to want to interfere with corporate policy.

There were times, however, when almost everyone in the Netherlands was willing to stand up and show his defiance of the Germans. On June 29, 1940, Bernhard's twenty-ninth birthday, people from all across the country donned carnations to demonstrate their loyalty to the Prince. German soldiers ripped the carnations off clothing, occasionally to their regret. Some people had hidden razor blades in the flower.

Ironically, the people of the Netherlands were loyal to Bernhard, but English authorities questioned his loyalty to the Allied cause. Despite the personal recommendation of King George that Bernhard be allowed to work in Intelligence, the request was turned down. "The War Ministry won't have you, Your Royal Highness," King George's secretary told Bernhard, "because you are German. His Majesty did his best, but he can't force you down their throats."

A friend of Bernhard's recommended him for the Air Ministry, but he too returned with disturbing news: "The Air Marshal says, 'A leopard does not change his spots.' "

It was more than just Bernhard's being German that cooled the British authorities. He was, after all, married to the Crown Princess of the Netherlands. British Intelligence knew about his stint with the League for Air Sports and his former membership in the SS, about his loose tongue with the Nazi Langenheim; they might even have known about his activities in behalf of I. G. Farben, and they did not trust him. Later, reportedly under pressure from Wilhelmina, the British relented and Bernhard was admitted into the councils of war planning and was provided access to important secrets.

Meanwhile Juliana, her children, and their entourage had settled into a large six-bedroom house at 14 Lansdowne Road in a wooded area outside Ottawa. The house overlooked a lovely, picturesque Canadian lake, and its remoteness satisfied Colonel Sesink's insistence on security. Juliana immediately endeared herself to the Canadian people by saying how much she enjoyed her new home. "When you forget something upstairs at Soestdijk," she remarked, "you have to walk a mile to get it."

But it was a radio speech to the Canadian people, June 17, 1940, that made the most enduring impression on her hosts: "Please do not regard me as too much of a stranger, now that I set foot on these shores, which my own ancestors helped to discover, to explore and to settle. . . .

"And then there are my two children. You will see them among you. Indeed you will see them quite often for we do not like to lock ourselves up. It is just not in our nature. I hope you will be kind to them. I am their mother and therefore I rather think they are very sweet children. Above all things they smile quite easily. Please give them your smile and they will be happy and they will ask for very little more. That I think is about all there is to tell."

Juliana was often visited by Princess Alice, Queen Emma's sister and one of Beatrix's godmothers, whose husband, the Earl of Athlone, was Canada's Governor General. There was a variety of other guests, official and otherwise, and many duties to perform, but Juliana knew the real action was taking place in England and on the Continent. Her major contribution, it was very clear, would be simply staying alive and preserving the heirs to the Dutch throne.

Each day in Canada the differences in personal style between Juliana and her mother became more plainly evident. Juliana was warmer, less demanding of those around her, less prone to ostentatious displays. Most people would never consider not bowing when introduced to Wilhelmina, but Juliana wanted none of it, except on official occasions. Juliana occasionally did her own grocery shopping in Ottawa, a tall, ordinary woman virtually indistinguishable from other shoppers in the stores. Of course, an alert observer watching closely might have spotted Colonel Sesink lurking in the background. He kept a personal eye on Juliana just as he had during her honeymoon; other security men were assigned to Beatrix and Irene.

Juliana constantly felt inconvenienced in Canada by her inability to keep a cook. One problem was that the royal family was accustomed to eating six meals a day, not three, so the hours were terrible. Finally Bernhard intervened with the Dutch army and had a cook assigned to the house in Ottawa. At least, Bernhard reasoned, the man could not quit. Unfortunately, he soon developed an ulcer and had to be replaced. Bernhard next intervened with the Dutch navy and had a cook from one of the submarines attached to the household in Canada. This man had seen so much wartime action, however, almost twenty months continuously underwater, that his hands shook whenever he tried to measure ingredients, and he was constantly dropping dishes. He also was in awe of the royal family, and when he was told Wilhelmina was coming for a visit, he climbed into bed and refused to stir for four days.

Beatrix began taking classes at home and Juliana was entranced by the way she signed her school papers: Trix of Orange.

Bernhard first visited Juliana in Canada in June 1941, and they made a quick tour of the United States together. They visited Holland, Michigan, America's "Tulip Capital," where Juliana was presented with an honorary law degree by Hope College, and ended their brief tour as guests of those famous Dutch-Americans in the White House, Eleanor and Franklin Roosevelt.

The next summer, 1942, Wilhelmina and Bernhard paid separate visits to Canada. During Bernhard's visit Juliana and the family moved to a much bigger house on Acacia Avenue in Ottawa, and when Wilhelmina came she and Juliana spent part of the summer vacationing in the Berkshires in Massachusetts. That same summer Wilhelmina delivered an important historic speech in Washington, D.C., in which she promised the Dutch East Indies its independence. Although it was later denied by

Wilhelmina, many Dutch people were probably correct when they said the speech was delivered under pressure from President Roosevelt. Roosevelt was certainly in a position to apply pressure: the Netherlands was occupied by the Germans, and America represented the House of Orange's only opportunity to recapture what it had lost. Regardless, what Wilhelmina delivered was *only* a speech, as proved by the ferocious tenacity with which the Dutch would later try to hold their colony.

Bernhard returned to Canada in January 1943 to await the birth of his third child, and he promptly caught the mumps. It was an illness that the royal family later credited with saving his life. He had been scheduled to recross the Atlantic in a B-25 Mitchell bomber, but could not catch the flight because he was sick. The B-25 Mitchell was a new series of airplane, and nine of the first twelve that attempted a transatlantic flight went down without survivors. When Bernhard was healthy enough to make the trip, it was in a safer aircraft.

Princess Margriet was born on January 19, 1943, at Civic Hospital in Ottawa. The Canadian Parliament passed a special law declaring extraterritorial the four-room suite Juliana occupied, in order to guarantee there would be no question about the baby's nationality. *Margriet* means "daisy," the flower that had become the symbol in the Netherlands for all those who had perished in the war.

No cannons boomed in the Netherlands to announce the birth of Margriet, but there were quiet celebrations nonetheless. A woman in Zeeland wrote to her imprisoned son, "Our Julie has had her baby." It was a crude attempt at deception, but the Nazi censor let it go through. He even scribbled on the letter, "The name is Margriet."

The people in Holland were continuing to struggle as

best they could. When in February 1941 a gang of young Nazis entered the Jewish section of Amsterdam, they were soundly thrashed by young Jews who had formed themselves into Action Groups, and one of the Nazis, Hendrik Koot, was killed. A total of 425 Jews were arrested in retaliation; many were tortured, all were killed. Underground organizations, chiefly the Communist Party, began to organize a strike of public workers. The strike was successful beyond their wildest hopes. Workers all over the nation walked off their jobs, paralyzing production. Heinrich Himmler himself stepped into the turmoil with a typically brutal hand, and ordered the increased use of torture and the arrest of one thousand strikers. But still it did not end. Increasing numbers of workers stayed off the job. German police roamed the streets shooting strikers, but this by itself did not stop the protesters. Instead, it was a realization that they were outgunned and that a different form of struggle was necessary that finally persuaded the Dutch people to return to work. But the hatred of the German oppressors had been multiplied a hundredfold. The lies about racial superiority, about the "New Europe," and about National Socialism, all had been forever exposed for those who had witnessed Nazism's true face.

In England Wilhelmina had been kept well appraised of the suffering in the Netherlands by the numerous people lucky enough to escape. Her religion gave her consolation: "In the silence and solitude of my exile," she wrote, "where all the reports I received told of misfortunes and hardship and sorrow, and where I suffered so much myself, I was often led to compare the fate of the Netherlands and myself to the experience of Job at the time of his adversity.

"At first I was unable to detach myself from the gloom

of the Book of Job. Then I realized how Job had had to find the right attitude to God and life in the only possible way, by passing through an ordeal. When he had found it, God accorded him a new period of prosperity as a visible token of his loving care in matters of this life as well as the next."

Juliana's best friend in Canada was Martine Roell, who had come from the Netherlands to England with the Crown Princess, and then aboard the *Sumatra* to Canada. Martine had left her husband, William, behind in Holland, and he was arrested by the Nazis and sentenced to die in 1942. Bernhard persuaded his mother, Baroness Armgard, with whom he was communicating by code through BBC classical music broadcasts, to intervene in Roell's behalf with the Duke of Mecklenburg, a friend of Göring's and a man known to have Hitler's ear. Part of the concern for William Roell was that he was an agent for the House of Orange charged with keeping track of its property. Baroness Armgard, who was living in Germany, received her son's message, but her intervention with the Duke of Mecklenburg was unsuccessful and William Roell was executed. Martine Roell continued to live with Juliana at 541 Acacia Avenue, Rockcliffe.

After the war, the Duke of Mecklenburg asked Bernhard for personal help. He was almost penniless. "The Prince of the Netherlands," said Bernhard, "will be pleased to give the Duke of Mecklenburg-Schwerin exactly the same amount of assistance as the Duke gave to his friend William Roell."

But Juliana, and especially Martine, could not at the time have known.

Juliana enjoyed attending motion pictures in Canada. She usually reserved seats in advance, but occasionally she would stand, unrecognized, in line to buy a ticket. She noted the difference between the Netherlands and Canada with mixed pleasure: few in Canada even recognized her, much less knew the power and wealth to which she was heir; in Holland she would have been mobbed by admirers.

Juliana's neighbors on Acacia Avenue remember her warmly. When Mrs. John Graham was about to have her third child, she recalls Juliana's offering to take care of the first two. Another time she remembers walking into Woolworth's and seeing Juliana sipping coffee at the counter. When Mrs. Graham gave birth to a boy, Juliana looked at the infant and cried. "It seemed a son was very important to her," Mrs. Graham said.

The years in Canada would always be treasured by Juliana, but in certain ways they were very puzzling to her. She believed, as Wilhelmina had, that royal children should have more contact with average citizens, that it was good to be more democratic, that the days of arrogant, insulated monarchy were past; but Juliana fell short of her goals for the same reason her mother had: what Juliana believed were revolutionary innovations for the time were ridiculed and sneered at as too conservative by a new generation. Thus, sending Beatrix and Irene to public school in Canada failed to accomplish its announced purpose when the children could clearly be observed being escorted by Sesink's ubiquitous guards. Juliana and Wilhelmina seemed to lend credence to Boswell's assertion that a person should come to the Netherlands if he was certain the world was about to end, because there everything happened fifty years later.

A great deal of the time Juliana was not in Canada. She met Dutch warships that called in North America, visited Dutch families, lobbied her friends Franklin and Eleanor for reconstruction aid for Holland. Juliana also paid official visits to the Dutch Antilles Islands in the Caribbean, and to Surinam. She could not perform royal duties with the regal, distant air Wilhelmina exuded, but she had a touch of humanity and vulnerability people could sense.

Some of Juliana's statements were quoted on Radio Orange: "A people who have fought for centuries against invaders and who have wrenched the very earth from the sea itself can never be conquered." This was an allusion to a popular saying in Holland, "God created the world, but the Dutch made the Netherlands," referring to the great amount of land people had reclaimed from the sea.

Margriet was christened in Ottawa, and Wilhelmina flew over from London for the occasion. President Roosevelt and the Earl of Athlone were godfathers, and Queen Mary and Martine Roell the godmothers. Wilhelmina went on to Hyde Park for a weekend with the Roosevelts, and then returned to Canada to find the wife of Chiang Kai-shek staying with Juliana. Shortly thereafter Wilhelmina moved to a country house in Great Britain near South Mimms. She gave as her reason the polluted air of Stubbings, but she almost died because of the move. A German bomb killed several of her guards and damaged the house where she was living.

Juliana flew to England in September 1944, leaving the three children in Canada. She expected soon to be in Holland, but the disastrous Battle of Arnhem dashed that hope and led to the terrible winter of 1944–45. People in the Netherlands starved in the streets. Others froze to death. Many who survived did so by eating tulip bulbs. And the Germans became even more barbaric: torture chambers and firing squads worked overtime; the unburied dead were piled one on top of another in Amsterdam; and in all, tiny Holland had about the same number of fatalities as the United States. There was scarcely a person in the nation who did not lose a relative.

In England Juliana worked with the Swiss and Swedish Red Cross to arrange food shipments to the Netherlands, but the Nazis refused to let them in until railway workers ended their strike. The workers continued to stay out.

Perhaps the worst suffering was in Putten, "the village of widows." The Germans dragged the men out of their homes and killed them.

Juliana spent Christmas in England and was with her mother when she concluded her Christmas Day broadcast: "It would show a lack of reverence to conclude with prayer in these circumstances, over the radio, and yet, while we can think of nothing but the nameless distress of our people, our thoughts often pass into prayer unnoticed. God only knows how many hands are folded, certainly a great many more than we think. I feel united with you in spirit, remembering all the deported men and all those who are sighing in prisons and torture camps, all mothers and children and all the others who suffer from hunger and cold, all the weak and the sick, our heroes of the Resistance, our forces on land, at sea and in the air, our merchant seamen and fishermen and the severely tried members of the empire in the tropics. May God's blessing be with you, wherever you are."

Juliana flew to the United States in January 1945 to ask President Roosevelt for postwar aid for the Netherlands. She saw the President again in March, shortly before his death. After the January visit, Juliana returned to Canada and a reunion with the children.

It was clear she would soon be able to return to Holland. Each day Juliana received encouraging secret reports from Wilhelmina outlining the rapid disintegration of

German forces. None of her children had any memories whatever of their country—Margriet had never even been there—so Juliana spent long hours telling them about the Netherlands and what they could expect life to be like. Juliana also held a series of good-bye parties for her Canadian friends, people who would be genuinely sorry to see her leave. But Juliana intended to leave something behind.

Ottawa became one of the great tulip cities of the world—a two-week Tulip Festival is held every May—because each year since 1945 Juliana has sent a gift of fifteen thousand tulip bulbs to the Canadian capital. Two million tulip bulbs are now planted annually in Ottawa, representing a booming industry that owes its existence to the Queen of the Netherlands. But flowers are not the only things that remind visitors to Ottawa that Juliana once lived there. A street has been named for her, and the Queen Juliana Hall at Rockcliffe Park Public School. People still drive by the house on Lansdowne Road, named *Nooit Gedacht*—"Never Thought"—by Juliana because she never imagined she would live so far from the Netherlands.

Juliana, again without the children, returned to Great Britain in April 1945. She and Wilhelmina were eager to arrive in the Netherlands the moment the Germans were out so that there would be no leadership vacuum. Finally it was agreed they would arrive on April 30, Juliana's thirty-sixth birthday, and all preparations had been completed when the flight was canceled by bad weather. It was on April 30, with Russian troops relentlessly closing in on his bunker, that Adolf Hitler killed himself.

Two days later Juliana and Wilhelmina returned home.

8

Long live our Queen!

No large, cheering crowds greeted the Queen and the Crown Princess when they arrived at a nearly deserted airport in the Netherlands on a military plane on May 2. A car sped them to Breda, where they were immediately occupied with the very large tasks of establishing a government, restoring order, and getting Holland back on its feet. Wilhelmina seemed to many in the country to have performed most admirably during the war, and they looked to her for guidance. For the moment elections were out of the question, so a cabinet was formed that represented various segments of society.

The armistice was signed on May 4, but there were many areas in the Netherlands where it was still not safe to travel. Individual Nazis, especially fanatical SS men, were choosing to fight it out rather than surrender, and Dutch clean-up squads were organized to capture them before they could wreak too much mayhem. Nevertheless, many people in Holland were killed after the armistice.

Bernhard had been reunited for the first time in six years with his mother, Baroness Armgard, and his brother,

Aschwin, at Bad Driburg in Germany shortly after it was liberated by the Americans, but now he had set himself and his staff up at Het Oude Looe to supervise mopping-up operations. His choice of Wilhelmina's favorite palace as a headquarters outraged the Queen, and it was months before she would talk with him civilly. In reality, she had first stated she wanted the palace burned to the ground because the Nazis had stayed there, and only later, when memories flooded back, did she change her mind.

Bernhard was active in working out the Nazi surrender in the Netherlands with General Blaskowitz, the German commander in Holland. The remarks Bernhard made about Blaskowitz enraged many Dutch Resistance fighters. "I felt sorry," he said, "for the German general in Holland at the time of the surrender. He was a gentleman of the old school who had fought as such. The old boy had had a row with Hitler and resigned. At the end, Hitler recalled him and sent him to command in Holland because he knew it would be the first to go. Having seen everything collapse around me in the May Days I knew how he felt."

Blaskowitz would commit suicide after the Russians charged him with war crimes.

Juliana accompanied Wilhelmina to many towns and cities that were considered safe by Dutch security forces. Their reception was always extremely enthusiastic; the people of Holland were glad to have them back. Citizens stood on the sides of roads waving and cheering, happiness and relief etched on their faces, bits of orange attached to their clothing, bouquets of tulips in their hands. Wilhelmina, especially, had served as a symbol of national identity, and the people poured out affection for her.

Juliana was now receiving intensified firsthand instruction in how to be a Queen. Wilhelmina had already spoken about abdicating, and she wanted her daughter prepared for her responsibilities; in fact, twice before she actually did step down, she permitted Juliana to reign as Regent. The excuse given was that Wilhelmina was ill, but many people in the Netherlands believe the illnesses were a cover to give Juliana experience. Juliana's own health was excellent and would so continue: not once since she became Queen has she been reported sick. She had always been a sturdy, healthy Dutch woman, a medical joy for her physicians.

Wilhelmina reshuffled her court upon returning from England. The political views of some previous members were hardly in keeping with the antifascist spirit prevalent in the days following liberation, and those members had to be replaced, as did a few who were too old and sick. The new court was not composed of members arguing for radical change, however, and it remained as stern and unsmiling as ever.

Juliana was president of the Dutch Red Cross at this time, although she was more than the figurehead her father had been. She also worked closely with the Netherlands National Reconstruction organization. Often she appeared outside the residence in Breda to greet the seemingly endless lines of people who filed past, people who simply wanted to see a member of the House of Orange to assure themselves that the German nightmare was over. Citizens felt they could talk with Juliana and often did, something only the most bold would dare with Wilhelmina. It was this accessibility in the years just ahead that made the majority of Dutch people eager for Wilhelmina to abdicate in her daughter's favor. Mainly it was older Dutch citizens who preferred the Queen remain on.

Juliana flew to New York City in July where she met Beatrix, Irene, and Margriet, who had been brought from Ottawa by Martine Roell and Colonel Sesink. They sailed aboard the *Queen Mary* to England, vacationed for several days, and then flew in two C-47's to an airport near Apeldoorn. Juliana and Margriet went in one plane, Beatrix and Irene in the other, to assure that a crash would not kill all of the heirs to the throne of the Netherlands. Bernhard greeted his family emotionally at the airport, throwing a bear hug around Juliana.

Beatrix was not impressed by what she first saw of wartorn Holland as the limousine transferred the royal family from the airport to their home at Soestdijk Palace. "I thought Holland always looked neat and tidy," she said, unable to comprehend what her countrymen had suffered.

The first meal at Soestdijk was not a pleasant one. Bernhard made it clear the children had picked up too many bad habits in Canada. He became angry with Margriet when she beat a spoon on her plate, reprimanded Irene for sitting on her foot, and complained about Beatrix's talking with food in her mouth. The children did not like the meal of fillet of sole, which further aggravated Bernhard.

"Can't we have steak and ice cream?" Beatrix asked.

"The German soldiers," Juliana explained, "stole most of the animals in Holland during the war, and planes killed a lot, and now many of our farms have been flooded so the farmers can't grow anything."

Bernhard was convinced the children had been raised in too lax an atmosphere in Ottawa and were sorely in need of discipline. On the first day at Soestdijk Beatrix forgot to take her spaniel puppy for a walk, the dog messed a valuable bedroom carpet, and Bernhard forbade her to have candy for a week.

Juliana thought the children had benefited from their stay in Canada and was anxious because there were no playmates at Soestdijk. Juliana was trying in her own way to give the children the companionship she herself had missed while growing up, so she telephoned a school authority and said she would like to give a party for every child from grades one through six in the three neighboring villages. Six hundred youngsters showed up.

"Yesterday I heard you address my secretary as Cees," Bernhard accused Beatrix.

"But I've talked to him at least three times, Daddy," she answered. "Why can't I call him by his first name?"

"Because he happens to be much older than you. Because this is not Canada."

Bernhard took the trappings of royalty more seriously than Juliana. He was known to be outraged with servants when he found a spot on a cup or smudges on a glass. At first glance this would seem a trait that would have endeared him to Wilhelmina, but the old Queen was suspicious of her daughter's husband. Some people in the Netherlands believe she sensed in Bernhard qualities possessed by the rascally Prince Henry. Regardless, neither Bernhard nor his ancestors had ever experienced anything like the reverence and adulation accorded the House of Orange as a matter of course, and he seemed unable to cope with the acclaim in Juliana's relaxed manner.

Juliana herself still dreamed of a male heir. She knew how much he would mean to Wilhelmina and the people of the Netherlands. She was only thirty-six years old and her excellent health made the goal seem attainable. She would breast-feed the new baby, as she had the three girls, and he would be raised in the same modern way.

In September 1945 Juliana enrolled Beatrix and Irene in the Boeke School. Boeke was a former anarchist known for his progressive methods of teaching, and nobility in the Netherlands criticized Juliana for exposing the children to him. Each day the two girls were driven to class in a chauffeured limousine containing two detectives, who then waited outside the school, looking conspicuous, until the Princesses were ready to return to Soestdijk. Children at the Boeke School were not given grades.

The detectives were probably necessary, given the danger of kidnapping, and so too was the limousine, but they were barriers to the "normal" upbringing Juliana so wanted for her daughters. Later, when Juliana seemed to lose control over the Princesses, she would be criticized by the nobility for being too lenient, and by others for not having permitted enough freedom.

Bernhard was soon disillusioned with the education being given Beatrix and Irene at the Boeke School, and he had them transferred to a special school at Baarn. The atmosphere at the new school was much more formal.

Juliana seemed to be much more attuned to the requirements of the times than Bernhard, despite all his worldly experience. Juliana recognized that attitudes were changing and people in the few nations still ruled by monarchies wanted their royalty to show a more human side. Thus, when Beatrix casually told a reporter how much she enjoyed chewing gum, Juliana and Bernhard responded differently.

"After all," Juliana reasoned to her husband, "Trix couldn't know it was a newspaper reporter."

"But she is much too casual about such things," Bernhard shot back. "For instance, it is quite intolerable the way she—and her sisters—burst into my study at all hours without knocking."

Throughout the marriage Bernhard seemed unhappy about the salary he received from the state. Evidently Juliana also felt her compensation was inadequate, but she worked behind the scenes to improve the situation rather than going public with her complaints. "Quite apart from the economic difficulties of our countries," Bernhard told a writer from *Collier's*, "we princes have financial problems of our own." Bernhard's principal financial problem, it would later be suggested, was that Juliana would not dip into her enormous private fortune to supplement the significant amount he already received from the people of the Netherlands.

Juliana was exempt from any inheritance taxes whatever, so the vast fortune left by her mother—except for grants to others—was passed along intact. Beatrix also will be exempt from inheritance taxes, but her three sisters will not be.

Shortly before Beatrix started school, she asked her governess, "We're rich, aren't we?"

"Yes, you are."

"Well," said Beatrix, "I can't say I'm sorry."

Juliana and Bernhard took numerous holidays in 1946. It was perhaps the last year she had before the press of royal duties would require that she remain in the Netherlands.

Christmas, 1946, was a happy time at Soestdijk. Wilhelmina decided to dress up as Santa Claus as a treat for the children. The man attaching the whiskers to her face became so nervous he almost fainted. When she finally burst in on the children crying, "Ho! Ho! Ho!" Beatrix said, "Why, it's Granny in a dressing gown."

Princess Marijke, Juliana's fourth daughter, was born on February 18, 1947, at Soestdijk Palace. The cannons again roared, not 101 times, as Juliana had hoped, but 51. *Marijke* is a popular form of Maria, and in later years the Princess insisted on being called by her second name, Christina.

When the news of Greet Hofmans was finally released to the Dutch people, the nation split largely along sexual lines. Most women sympathized with Juliana, believing she was right to take any chance that might save her child's sight. Many men thought she should continue to pursue conventional medical cures. The controversy over the faith healer drove a deep wedge between Juliana and Bernhard, but there already had been fissures and splits: over raising the children, over Bernhard's requests for additional money, over Bernhard's freewheeling life-style that embarrassed Juliana and threatened to explode in scandal, and over Juliana's own very deep religious convictions as opposed to Bernhard's more materialistic outlook.

Wilhelmina once wrote, "I set no store by worldly goods," words that seemed strange coming from the richest woman on earth, but Juliana adopted them as her own. Later, when Juliana was consulted on business deals involving millions of dollars, dollars Bernhard craved, the "no store by worldly goods" standard was incomprehensible to him.

The year 1947 was one of preoccupation with Holland's deteriorating position in the Dutch East Indies, where a successful revolt had been a long time coming. Juliana and Wilhelmina, as they consulted their ministers and generals, must have known the tide was running against them. As early as the seventeenth century the Dutch had murdered natives on the Banda Islands whose rulers would not make deals with them, rather than surrender Holland's world monopoly on mace and nutmeg. In 1825 William I began to crush a revolt that ultimately took 200,000 Javanese lives and 15,000 Dutch lives. Just before World War II, as Frank Huggett pointed out in *The Modern Netherlands,* "the Indies were estimated to have supplied 90 per cent of the world's production of quinine, 86 per cent of the world's pepper, 75 per cent of its kapok, 37 per cent of its rubber, 28 per cent of its coconut-palm products, 19 per cent of its tea, and 17 per cent of its tin as well as sugar, coffee, oil and most of the world's cigar wrappers."

When the Japanese occupied the Dutch East Indies during World War II, they promoted nationalism for their own sinister reasons. Even after Japan surrendered, its troops, under order of the Allies, were responsible for ruling until other countries could take over. Many of the defeated Japanese encouraged additional nationalistic sympathies among the East Indies forces headed by Sukarno. Soon there was a full-scale war raging: the Netherlands had 20,000 troops in the East Indies at the end of 1945; there were 150,000 by July 1947. These troops, involved in bitter battle, were not always willing to fight with the memory of World War II still fresh in their minds, and often morale was not high. Most of the world, in addition, was demanding that Holland sue for peace, but the country fought on, inflicting heavy casualties.

Wilhelmina's popularity was on the wane. Although she wholeheartedly supported the war effort, her Washington, D.C., speech in 1942 was remembered and blamed for instilling "false hope" in the Indonesians. Of course, the Indonesians had been exploited by the Dutch for 350 years and needed no encouragement from Wilhelmina to revolt, but such was the temper in Holland that she was selected to bear responsibility.

Often when a nation loses a war, the leader is replaced. Although Wilhelmina pleaded advancing age and declining health, the chief reason for her decision to abdicate was the hopeless situation in the East Indies. It was believed that with the loss of that great colony, the Netherlands would be doomed to decades of austerity and belt tightening. Also, proud old Wilhelmina did not want to be the one to sign papers that amounted to a surrender.

On the ninety-ninth anniversary of William III's becoming King—May 12, 1948—Wilhelmina went on radio to tell the Dutch people that she intended to abdicate. Juliana was immediately made Regent so that she could gain additional on-the-job experience, and she soon was the focus of intense press attention. *Time* magazine described her listening to a May 1948 speech delivered by Winston Churchill:

Juliana sat leaning forward, her firm chin firmly planted in her firm hand, squinting a little, nodding a little from time to time as she followed with an obvious effort Churchill's not very difficult line of thought. Her mien was strikingly familiar; it recalled the American matron who had learned at Bryn Mawr that an active interest in public affairs was the duty of an educated, responsible woman, and who was not going to use motherhood merely as an excuse for shirking her duty.

The Bryn Mawr alumna would buy tickets for a lecture on economics by the late John Maynard Keynes and would go in much the same spirit as Juliana went to hear Churchill. Just as the Bryn Mawr alumna would bring her husband, so Juliana brought Bernhard. He sat there looking as if he would rather be at a country club, but had been almost reconciled to the educational occasion.

Wilhelmina's historic abdication took place on September 4, 1948, in the magnificent Moses Room in Dam Palace in Amsterdam. Erect as ever, accompanied by her court, Wilhelmina listened as the director of the Queen's Secretariat read the act of abdication. Then she stepped forward and signed it with a firm hand. The abdication was witnessed by just twenty-six people, all of them specially selected by Wilhelmina.

Precisely at noon the huge double French doors leading to a flower-bedecked second-floor balcony at Dam Palace were flung open and Wilhelmina and Juliana came out

hand in hand. Thousands of people wearing orange rib-
bons waited below, and they listened in silence as Wilhelmina, dressed in a sensible powder-blue suit and gray
felt hat, delivered her speech of abdication. Juliana, wearing gray with a pillbox hat, struggled to choke back the
tears.

Then came a moment no one in the crowd would have
wanted to miss. When Wilhelmina was finished she took
a step back from the microphones, thrust her fist in the
air, waved it in a wide arc, and cried "Long live our
Queen!" The big crowd roared back mightily, "Long
live our Queen!" Again and again Wilhelmina, swinging
her fist over her head like a one-armed hammer thrower
winding up the ball, shouted, "Long live our Queen!"
and each time the echo came back the same. An American observer witnessing the scene said it reminded him of
a college coed leading cheers, that he kept telling himself
it was childish and corny, but somehow he was deeply
moved.

Wilhelmina kissed Juliana and, as Alden Hatch described, "pushed her gently forward." It was time for
Queen Juliana's first address to the nation: "I thank you,
dear Mother," she said softly and tentatively, "for intro-
ducing me this way. I feel that it is a great sorrow that in
the future we will have to do without your wisdom and
experience and, above all, yourself as our Queen. . . ."

As soon as Juliana's speech was ended, and without a
cue, the crowd burst into the strains of the Dutch national
anthem, "Wilhelmus van Nassau."

Bernhard, elegant in an admiral's uniform, accompanied
by the three oldest Princesses, clad in red with blue hair-
bows, joined Juliana and Wilhelmina on the balcony. The
crowd was a sea of noise and emotion. Dutch government
officials and officials from the colonies, including one

from Indonesia, joined the royal family on the balcony. All of this lasted only ten minutes, but it seemed to many who were present that it had gone on the entire afternoon.

Juliana, Bernhard, and the three oldest daughters had yet one more royal duty to perform this day. At 4 P.M. they rode in a horse-drawn coach through the packed streets of Amsterdam to receive the cheers of the city's people. One Dutch girl in the crowd was overheard saying to a friend: "Look at Trix waving. She has more poise than her mother."

Wilhelmina, shrewd to the last, made her final acts as Queen those she considered most important. She signed a constitutional amendment authorizing union between the Netherlands and Indonesia, but it was far too late and a gesture without meaning because Indonesia wanted nothing less than independence and was in a position to get it. Wilhelmina also signed a bill granting herself a pension.

On September 4, 1948, the day Wilhelmina led cheers for the Queen, Juliana had not yet been formally inaugurated, although she did officially and by law become Queen the moment her mother abdicated. The inauguration itself was scheduled for September 6. Just before this took place Juliana attended an exhibition on "The Netherlands Woman, 1898–1948." Wearing a green print dress and sandals—Juliana seldom dresses extravagantly—she made a few remarks that today would be regarded as feminist, a movement, incidentally, which she supports: "In the past fifty years woman has finally had courage to work herself in those spheres for which she had formerly been deemed too delicate."

The inauguration was almost at hand when Juliana was presented with a mammoth cake, multilayered, that completely covered a five-foot table. It was a gift from the armed forces, whose men had cut back on their own rations to save enough to purchase the confection. Juliana called it a "monument" that "should go to a museum." Instead it was cut with an officer's sword and Beatrix, Irene, and Margriet each had large pieces.

There were parties and balls all over the Netherlands the night before the inauguration. The only monarch the nation had known in the twentieth century had stepped down, and her thirty-nine-year-old daughter was taking over. No one could have imagined the incredibly stormy years that lay ahead for the new Queen.

9

Listen, lady, my job is to get you out of here,
and if possible with your clothes on.

SEPTEMBER 6, 1948, was a day that belonged to Juliana. All of the Netherlands, and much of the world, focused attention on The Hague and the inauguration of the new monarch. *Newsweek's* London bureau chief, Fred Vanderschmidt, called the inauguration "the greatest show in postwar Europe," and few among the crowd of hundreds of thousands who showed up would have disagreed. Author Betty Hoffman described Juliana: "From her shoulders hung a cloak of scarlet velvet lined with white ermine and emblazoned with rampant lions in gold. Beneath it she wore a long tightly fitted sheath of heavy sapphire-blue silk against which blazed a magnificent jeweled sunburst necklace and the ribbon of the Military Order of William I. On her blonde head she wore a jeweled Juliet cap."

Royalty from all over the Continent were on hand, including Princess Margaret from Great Britain; and dozens of countries from around the globe sent representatives. The American delegation consisted of Herman Baruch, U.S. Ambassador to The Hague; Thomas J. Watson; and

Eleanor Wilson McAdoo. There were three thousand people crowded into Amsterdam's Nieuwe Kerk, where the
ceremony took place.

Juliana had become Queen the moment Wilhelmina
abdicated two days earlier, but the inauguration, with its
great pomp and ceremony, was considered the highlight
of festivities that had lasted a week. "I have been called,"
said Juliana in her inaugural address, "to a task so heavy
that no one who has the least notion of it would desire it,
but at the same time so splendid that I can only say: 'who
am I that I should be allowed to perform it?'"

Juliana went on to praise Wilhelmina: "My dear mother,
led by grandmother's love, wisdom and common sense,
you assumed the heavy task, supported later by father's
fine personality. I alone know, and then only partly, how
difficult a time you had in a world of conventional prejudices, particularly at first. With your keen vision and
strong feeling of unity with your fellow men you continued, however, to work for the good of the community.
I myself and everybody else always had the feeling you
were there like a rock. . . .

"In the hope that your modesty will not prevent you
from accepting it, the Knight's Cross of the Military
Willems Order, first class, will be presented to you as a
symbol of the culmination of your government and your
leadership during the dark years of war and oppression.
The signing of that decree will be my first act as Queen."

It was time to take the oath of office: "I swear to the
Netherlands people that I shall always uphold and maintain the Constitution. I swear that I shall defend and preserve with all My power the independence and the territory of the State; that I shall protect the general and
individual liberty and the rights of all My subjects
and that, for the maintenance and promotion of the gen-

eral and individual prosperity, I shall apply all the means which the laws place at My disposal, as it is the duty of a good Queen to do so. So help me God!"

Juliana was the twelfth member of the House of Orange to rule in the Netherlands.

The duties of Queen required that Juliana travel a great deal, and in the years ahead she paid official visits to France (1950), Great Britain (1950), the United States (1952), Norway (1953), Denmark (1953), Surinam and the Netherlands Antilles (1955), Luxembourg (1956), Sweden (1957), Belgium (1960), Austria (1962), Iran (1963), Thailand (1963), Mexico (1964), Canada (1967), and Ethiopia (1969). During the 1970s Juliana continued her travels, but although she represented Holland on her trips, there was continuous speculation that she also represented her own private interests, which by any accounting are significant.

Dutch journalist William Oltmans, well known in America for his investigations into the John Kennedy assassination, contends that Juliana is *not* the richest woman in the world. He is backed up by Holland's *Haagse Post,* which conducted a study of her finances. On the other hand, Dutch journalist Wim Klinkenburg estimates Juliana owns 5 percent of the stock of Royal Dutch Shell, and 5 percent, according to former U.S. Representative Wright Patman, would give Juliana a controlling interest in the corporation. Of course, Royal Dutch Shell is the largest corporation in the world outside the United States: 1977 sales of $39,680,211,000; assets of $36,021,735,000; and profits of $2,338,691,000. Anthony Sampson, in *The Seven Sisters,* explained one reason Shell was so profitable: "Shell oil was pumped from Shell oilfields into Shell tankers onto Shell refineries into Shell storage tankers and through Shell pipelines to Shell filling-stations."

On November 30, 1978, 5 percent of Royal Dutch Shell stock was worth $427,500,000. It is not surprising, as J. E. Hartshorn wrote in *Oil Companies and Governments,* that "the Dutch government, to the oil industry, acts as a very friendly neutral."

It has been reported that Juliana also holds stock in Exxon, the world's largest oil company, and there can be no doubt she owns much of the most valuable real estate and private property in Holland. Millions of dollars, for example, were recently spent to renovate Huis ten Bosch, which Princess Beatrix intends to make the royal residence if she becomes Queen. Juliana prefers Soestdijk Palace, which has marble floors and walls, priceless oil paintings, and gold furniture. One of her *used* cars—a Rolls-Royce Phantom—recently was purchased by St. Louis auto dealer Charles Schmitt for $280,000.

If Juliana did conduct business on behalf of private corporations during her trips abroad, there were others besides Royal Dutch Shell in Holland that were large enough to merit her attention. Unilever (1977 sales: $15,965,116,000) is the fourth-largest industrial corporation outside the United States, and Philips ($12,702,569,000) is fifth.

However much money Juliana has, it is certainly much more than she is credited with by conservative Dutch newspapers. Many of these, staunchly royalist, fear that if her true fortune were known, Dutch citizens might resent the large state expenditures she receives.

Although there is debate whether Juliana deserves the title of richest woman in the world, few people claim she devotes full time to the management of her fortune. She is aware of what is done with her investments—indeed, financial managers have to protect themselves by explaining what they intend to do in her behalf—but Juliana seems more preoccupied with religious pursuits than with finance.

The days immediately following the inauguration were personally trying for the new Queen. The Greet Hofmans affair was beginning to tear her marriage apart—at one point Juliana and Bernhard actually separated—and there was the impossible situation in Indonesia. It had helped bring down mighty Queen Wilhelmina, and it seemed altogether too much for Juliana to handle.

Until 1949 Indonesia had been a colony for 350 years, first under the Portuguese, then under the Dutch, briefly under Great Britain, then under the Dutch again, for a short time under the Japanese (1942–1945), and back again to the Dutch. What had started as the spice trade under the Portuguese soon became, under the direction of the more enterprising Dutch East India Company, a looter's paradise. Sugar, tea, coffee, and indigo were harvested by the natives and sold on world markets by the Dutch.

Juliana knew the history of Indonesia, but like British monarchs before her she could not believe the people really wanted independence. On August 17, 1945, after the defeat of the Japanese in World War II, a popular nationalist revolutionary named Sukarno proclaimed the Republic of Indonesia independent. His reasons were obvious: in 1945 Indonesia had about 100 million people, was the fifth-richest nation in the world in natural resources, had extremely fertile land and rich deposits of oil, tin, and bauxite; yet this sixth-largest country on earth was 93 percent illiterate and had a per capita income of $82 a year.

Indonesia was eloquent evidence of the evils that 350 years of colonial domination bring. In 1945 there were one university, two university professors, ten agricultural experts, less than one hundred engineers, and just over one hundred doctors. Almost as important, Indonesians wanted to regain their respect. They did not want to be hit in the face by a Dutch or Japanese soldier because they showed a "lack of respect."

With the Japanese defeated, Juliana—perhaps naively— believed that the three thousand islands that compose Indonesia would once again belong to the Netherlands. Sukarno did not think so, and for the next four years the poorly equipped peasants fought a war of liberation against tens of thousands of Dutch soldiers. Finally, on December 27, 1949, at Dam Palace in Amsterdam, the Dutch relinquished their colony. The papers were signed by Queen Juliana for the Netherlands and by Prime Minister Mohammed Hatta for Indonesia. The signing was an act that Wilhelmina had abdicated to avoid.

Soon there were many refugees streaming into Holland, chiefly people who had supported the colonial regime and now feared reprisals. The refugees vied with Dutch citizens for scarce jobs, and gradually racial tensions built up in the Netherlands. It was another problem with which Juliana had to deal, and its severity would be underlined when she later learned that one of the groups had plotted to kidnap her. But even at the outset there were numerous Dutch citizens, goaded on by opportunistic politicians, who claimed to find merit in South Africa's apartheid system. The major churches in South Africa were Dutch Reformed, whose historic Calvinism was drawn from seventeenth-century Holland. The Dutch Reformed Church believes in predestination, which leads easily to the concept of an elect or chosen people, which in turn can promote the idea of racial superiority. If Juliana felt any sympathy for apartheid, she did not voice it publicly. In fact, she donated money—the amount was never revealed—to the World Council of Churches' Program to

Combat Racism. Dutch residents of South Africa, in retaliation, collected money for South African troops fighting in Angola.

One of Juliana's first acts as Queen was to appoint Bern-
hard as Regent for Beatrix until she was eighteen. Had
Juliana died or become incapacitated before that time,
Bernhard would have ruled in his daughter's behalf.

Not everything going on at Soestdijk Palace was grim
during Juliana's first fifteen months as Queen. Bernhard's
dogs provided needed comic relief. Just before the inauguration, Juliana complained, "We have dogs all over the
place, including those two barking Sealyham terriers
which belong to my husband and which seem to recognize
no other master." Soon one of the Sealyhams bit Juliana,
which touched off a royal row. Juliana wanted the dog—
Martin—banished, but Bernhard refused even to apologize: "I was the only one who stood up for Martin. I
pointed out that he was only doing his duty in defending
my possessions. My wife should have been more careful."
After the inauguration, however, Bernhard's mother,
Baroness Armgard, was bitten by her son's large white
poodle, Bonzo.

Baroness Armgard was another potential source of concern for Juliana. She had moved into a castle in eastern
Holland and seemed particularly close to Beatrix, who
was siding with her father on the matter of Greet Hofmans.
There was always the possibility of a scandal where
Baroness Armgard was concerned. Reports circulated
that she may have been closer to the Nazi leadership than
she would like to admit, and that her son Aschwin had
not cut ties with the Nazis at age sixteen as he insisted. In
fact, it was said that Aschwin had been in the SA and
later the SS and had served the Germans throughout the
war. If true, the stories would not be welcomed in Holland, where even in 1949 German tourists asking direc-

tions were given a harsh answer: "You found your way in 1940. Find it now."

Juliana's becoming Queen had a different effect on her than on Bernhard. She drew inward into mysticism and religion; he became a super sales ambassador and world traveler. The combination was explosive. On a trip to Chile not long after the inauguration, Bernhard was photographed dancing with local beauties, but he dismissed the resulting headlines as "gossip." Bernhard said he and Juliana had a "hearty laugh" about the affair, although anyone who knows Juliana doubts that was her reaction.

More "gossip" came back to Juliana when Bernhard visited Argentina and was seen frequently in the company of Evita Perón. Bernhard thought it might be a good idea to "write down the rumors and the gossip and save them for [the] children. The stories will amuse the children and at the same time prepare them for the barbs they one day will have to endure. Perhaps they thereby will develop immunity to slanderous tongues, although one never completely succeeds in ignoring infamous gossip."

The rumors about Bernhard, besides not being something she wished he had written down for his children, troubled an already deeply worried Juliana. They came on top of the defeat in Indonesia and Marijke's blindness and pushed Juliana even closer to Greet Hofmans. Juliana's speeches increasingly contained mystical allusions and pacifist sentiments: "All armaments must be tossed into the sea," she asserted.

Juliana also was concerned with the speed with which Bernhard had used his elevated position to insinuate himself into business and government affairs. He was a member of the councils of the army, navy, and air force and had been appointed to the board of directors of KLM, the world's first airline. He seemed to have a head for business, but there were disturbing indications of how he conducted that business.

Juliana soon began putting her own imprint on the throne. She wore plain clothes, except for official occasions, often appearing in public dressed as any other Dutch housewife. She was frequently seen bicycling, her bodyguards following at a discreet distance. Juliana lacked glamour and poise, and when she spoke publicly it was with an awkward, stumbling, low, and sincere voice that carried a curious power because it was so simple. Anne O'Hare McCormick, writing in *The New York Times,* said Juliana's speeches were "fresh, unconventional and personal—not ready-made diplomatic addresses, not speeches from the Throne, but the utterances of an unpretentious woman of good sense and great goodwill."

An example of Juliana's power as a speaker came in 1950 after she was honored as "International Mother of the Year":

We, as mothers, have a very grave responsibility in these days. In the present world everybody is becoming more and more of a specialist. . . . We mothers, whether as career women or in the difficult job of housewives, are all of us specialists ourselves. But as mothers we have to see life as a whole. And so we can help the world to understand and to speak life's common language.

A mother is someone who has given life to someone else. She has to carry responsibility for those young lives. She simply cannot escape that; she has to shoulder it. And so she is exquisitely equipped to be the salt of the earth—your earth, which has become an interlocked community, which suffers no longer from being united, or rather suffers intolerably by being split up. . . .

But . . . we know that only too much of what is called love is in reality a very special pride, and that people ask only too often for the impossible from their children, in order to feel glorified in their own breed.

The daughters Juliana was trying to raise "democratically" posed a problem, "International Mother of the Year" or not. Beatrix had a habit of saying, "When I'm the Queen . . ." and none of the children could avoid noticing that they were very special people. Adults fawned over them. Children, taking advice from their parents, bowed and curtsied. Even little Marijke, a favorite of the Dutch people, was aware that "we are the only family in Holland with footmen."

Juliana had many other duties besides raising her four children: she had to be in regular and direct contact with her ministers, state secretaries, leading members of the States-General, Holland's ambassadors abroad, and her commissioners in the provinces. A great deal of time was spent reading and signing state documents. It was boring, tedious work, and Juliana did not enjoy being in the center of great affairs the way Wilhelmina had. She preferred to pray with Greet Hofmans and try better to understand Christ's teachings. Often in her speeches she urged people to live by Christian precepts, and her subjects believed she followed her own advice. Certainly the religious Juliana seemed an unlikely candidate to cause the stormy controversy that would engulf almost her entire reign.

An early controversy occurred shortly after she was inaugurated. Juliana refused to sign papers authorizing the death penalty for convicted war criminals, an action that had the effect of sparing their lives. War criminals had been put to death under Wilhelmina, and Juliana's refusal saddened many of the few remaining Jews in the Netherlands. Jewish citizens had suffered 112,000 of the 240,000 deaths inflicted by the Nazis; more than nineteen out of every twenty Jews in the country had been killed.

Juliana was far less imperious and demanding than

Wilhelmina, but she was still regarded with awe and fear by her servants. One day workmen arrived to install a television antenna for the servants at Soestdijk Palace. They were stopped short by a nervous butler: "But not this afternoon!" he pleaded. "Not at this hour! You will interrupt Her Majesty's nap and then she is likely to say we can't have any television set, not ever!"

Juliana visited the United States in April 1952 and was awarded an honorary LL.D. degree from Columbia University. She previously had received degrees from Hope College in Holland, Michigan; Princeton University; Mount Holyoke College; and Central College in Pella, Iowa. When Juliana arrived at Washington's National Airport, she was given a red-carpet welcome by President Truman, Bess Truman, and numerous members of the Cabinet. She was greeted with a twenty-one-gun salute at the airport, was driven through cheering crowds of government workers to the White House, and spent the night in the Rose Suite. The White House, of course, was a rather modest place compared to Soestdijk Palace, but Juliana seemed pleased to be a guest of the Trumans. Later she addressed a joint session of Congress: "The world is split into two parts, there are two magnetic poles of which one is positive—the one called democracy—and the other negative, indicating slavery. To my mind there is no doubt that if we could increase the energy radiated by the positive pole it would be impossible for the negative pole to withstand it."

An enthusiastic Congress heartily applauded the speech as anti-Communist, which indeed it was, but few members could have known that Juliana really believed in energy forces, especially those thrown off by planets.

There was a vacation in Sea Island, Georgia, a Detroit Tigers baseball game in Michigan, and stops in Philadelphia, Los Angeles, and San Francisco. The announced purpose of the trip was to cement goodwill between the Netherlands and the United States, and in this Juliana succeeded; but the real purpose was obtaining American aid for Holland. This also was brought about. Juliana concluded her trip with a stop in Canada to see wartime friends.

Several amusing incidents took place on the visit. At the baseball game in Detroit, where Juliana threw out the first ball, there was a terrific crunch of admiring people around Juliana as she tried to leave. Many of them were Dutch-Americans who wanted to get near her or touch her, but they were perhaps overly persistent. Juliana complained to a police officer that he was being too rough in pushing the crowd back. "Listen, lady," the cop said, "my job is to get you out of here, and if possible with your clothes on."

At Sea Island, Georgia, Bernhard found a sick duck. He tried to nurse it back to health with whiskey, but Colonel Sesink intervened and fed the bird dried corn. The duck promptly died, but Bernhard was deluged with congratulatory telegrams from bird lovers who felt he had performed a humanitarian gesture.

Juliana returned to the Netherlands on an airplane named the *Princess Beatrix*. She had intended to fly on the *Queen Juliana*, but that plane had crashed the week before she had begun the trip to America. After the crash people in the Netherlands urged Juliana not to fly at all, to travel by ship, but Bernhard overruled them: "If we change now it will give KLM a terrible black eye. It's out patriotic duty to go by plane. Besides it's perfectly safe."

The tradition of curtsying may largely have been eliminated from Juliana's court, along with other forms of pomp, but a party given by the Queen of the Netherlands was still a *royal* party, as she proved when she stopped in England on her way back from the United States. At a dinner she gave in London for King George, Juliana had almost *a ton* of gold and silver plate shipped from The Hague.

Bernhard had test-flown a Lockheed plane on the American trip and been guest at a stag luncheon thrown by Thomas J. Watson, Sr., of IBM. He was hailed by the press as a businessman and business ambassador *extraordinaire*. It was said that he never failed to return to the Netherlands with contracts for Dutch companies, which made him a subject of admiration for workers and industry alike. Bernhard was a very popular man in the Holland of 1952.

Bernhard's wife? Well, said conventional wisdom, she was rich, but more important, she was fortunate to be married to someone as sound as Bernhard. But then came a freezing, terror-filled night in late January 1953, and Juliana showed at her most heroic.

10

*Your faces all look so familiar to me! You
have been in my home many times.*

THE RECIPE was deadly: an abnormally high tide and
ferocious North Sea gale winds that approached one
hundred miles per hour. The result was a tidal wave, a
gigantic wall of water that slammed into Holland, Belgium, and Great Britain on the night of January 31, 1953,
and devastated large portions of those nations. England
called it the worst natural disaster in British history since
the great plague of 1664–1665. But it was much worse in
the Netherlands.

It was clear almost from the beginning that the flood
would be the worst in five centuries. Water surged
through gaping holes in the dikes, some as wide as a
hundred yards, all along Holland's coast, and entire
towns were inundated; by daybreak on February 1 the
known dead numbered 230.

Almost immediately Juliana took an active part in the
rescue work. She traveled by helicopter, plane, and boat
to the stricken areas, dressed in boots and an old coat.
She seemed such a good neighbor, so concerned, so eager
to help, that even foes of the monarchy conceded that she

was tremendous for morale. She was also tireless, but the destruction was so widespread that no one person could lend comfort everywhere. Former Queen Wilhelmina came out of seclusion to visit other besieged areas.

More than 40 percent of the Netherlands lies below sea level, and as reports were delivered to Juliana it became tragically clear that the disaster was enormous. The gale-driven waters reached twelve feet at some points, and dikes had broken at more than thirty points up and down the entire length of Holland's North Sea coast. Water had roared up the Rhine estuaries to Rotterdam and Dordrecht, crumbling dikes as it went, but the damage could have been even more vast. Workers braved dreadful weather conditions and were able to save The Hague, Leyden, and Delft.

Entire communities were simply swallowed up. The island of Walcheren was flooded, a grim replay of the time in 1944 when British bombers blasted the dikes to thwart a German threat to the Allied forces in Antwerp.

The United States, employing soldiers stationed in West Germany, organized a massive rescue operation in Holland. In addition, a disaster fund was started in New York City that had to operate around the clock to keep up with the food, clothing, and money that were pouring in. The problem that most concerned Juliana, however, was rescuing endangered survivors. "This is my home," said one farmer. "I would rather drown here."

The official death toll on February 2 stood at 955 in the Netherlands, but the rescue operation had begun to swing into gear. "Hundreds of ships," Daniel Schorr reported to *The New York Times,* "ranging from Queen Juliana's yacht to the humble herring trawler, were assembled in Dutch ports early this morning for an effort to evacuate tens of thousands of survivors trapped in flood-stricken

Zeeland, the islands to the south and the adjoining mainland."

Juliana rushed from one town to another, bringing food and clothing wherever she went. Dutch planes flew non-stop daylight airlifts, dropping rubber boats, and two thousand ships searched for stranded survivors. American and British helicopters joined the rescue effort. Home owners not affected by the flood were ordered to open their homes to victims.

Bernhard was in the United States at the time of the flood, attending the three-hundredth-anniversary celebration of a Dutch Reformed church. Soon he was on his way back to Holland, having been appointed president of a disaster fund headquartered at The Hague. When he arrived in the Netherlands, he plunged into relief work, but his efforts were greeted by controversy. "There was quite a bit of political pressure," Bernhard recalled, "put on the government to relieve me of my responsibilities. These people said they were afraid I'd get into trouble. They feared that if anything went wrong in handling the money, or if some of my decisions in the field turned out badly, I would get it in the neck and that would be bad for the monarchy. Well, I was quite ready to run the risk, and I never had any trouble on that account."

Most interesting about this account, which appeared in Alden Hatch's biography of Bernhard, was the fear "that if anything went wrong in handling the money . . ."

Juliana was in frequent consultation with her ministers. It was decided to forbid the export of potatoes, a crop heavily damaged by the flood, and to place a price ceiling on them to stop the speculation that already had begun. Rescue workers were given authority to evacuate flood victims forcibly, and emergency measures were readied to cope with the danger of epidemic.

The death toll rose to more than 1,000 on February 3, and to 1,269 on February 4. But it was not over yet. Fresh gales over the North Sea on February 4 unleashed a second terror on Holland, and additional tens of thousands of people were driven from their homes by the floods. Soldiers and volunteers fought high winds, freezing rain, and driving sleet to sandbag the dikes that still held. The story of the Dutch boy who held his finger in the dike is a fable, the invention of the nineteenth-century U.S. writer Mary Mapes Dodge, but a monument was erected for him in Spaarndam to attract American tourists. On February 4 thousands of Dutch boys worked alongside their fathers and mothers to try to hold back the sea.

Juliana seemed not to sleep at all, and her seventy-two-year-old mother was just as active. Juliana waded through water, slopped through mud; no place seemed too destitute to visit. She was winning the respect of the Dutch people, just as Wilhelmina had with her World War II broadcasts.

Property loss was staggering. Vast farmland was destroyed, livestock drowned by the thousands, entire buildings were swept away. Juliana could see, as she flew overhead, people clinging to rooftops, trees, and telephone poles. Many houses were totally underwater.

The death list reached 1,352 on February 5, but at least the winds had abated. Bernhard had raised some $3 million in disaster relief, and aid was still pouring in from private sources in the United States. All of it was pitifully little when compared to the destruction: $3 billion.

General Matthew B. Ridgway, Supreme Commander of Allied forces in Europe, flew to the Netherlands and offered his personal help, but it was rejected. Already there were some four thousand U.S. military personnel in Holland working on the rescue mission, and the nervous Dutch wanted no more involvement with foreign troops on their soil. The Americans had saved many lives, but they also revived old fears. Dutch volunteer workers said they were told their services were not needed because "the Yanks have taken over."

The Dutch did need financial assistance, and Juliana asked Secretary of State John Foster Dulles to put Holland back on its aid list. Just before the flood the United States had been informed that no more foreign aid was needed for the Netherlands. John Foster Dulles and Mutual Security Director Harold E. Stassen arrived at The Hague on September 6 and met with Juliana later that day. About the same time Juliana sent a message to President Eisenhower thanking him for American help.

The death toll ultimately climbed to more than two thousand, but the industrious Dutch people rebuilt as they had after the German occupation. There had been many heroes: an American helicopter pilot, half dead with exhaustion, flying "one more" mission and saving six lives; a Dutch schoolgirl, ten years old, saving her own and her sister's life by keeping a rubber raft afloat in the stormy waters; but especially, in the eyes of many, Juliana, who had seemed a source of infinite strength throughout the ordeal.

On November 8, 1953, Juliana stood proudly atop a new dike to celebrate the final damming-out of the North Sea waters. She delivered a speech in her low, shy voice, telling the Dutch people about projects already in the works which she hoped would make future disastrous flooding impossible.

Bernhard, meanwhile, had continued to become involved in international affairs. Although Juliana was more concerned about raising her daughters and praying with Greet Hofmans, she was interested in the meeting her husband was instrumental in organizing at the Bilderberg Hotel in eastern Holland between May 29 and May 31, 1954. Out of the meeting came an annual affair called the Bilderberg Conference, perhaps Bernhard's greatest and most puzzling achievement. Each year since 1954, until 1976, a multination conclave that named itself the Bilderberg met for a long weekend in such secrecy that even trusted members of the press were excluded. Bernhard was chairman of the Bilderberg, and members have included such prestigious people as Hugh Gaitskell, McGeorge Bundy, Jean Monnet, David Rockefeller, Walt Whitman Rostow, Harold Wilson, Dean Acheson, Dean Rusk, Jacob Javits, Christian Herter, J. William Fulbright, Robert McNamara, George Ball, Henry Heinz II, Henry Ford III, William Moyers, Lester Pearson, Pierre Mendes-France, Pierre Trudeau, and Stavros Niarchos.

Bringing together the elite of the corporate and political establishment to exchange "their views on the state of the world" under his chairmanship was quite an accomplishment for Bernhard and lent great luster to his reputation. Juliana had to be impressed by her husband's initiative, although her life from approximately the 1954 founding of the Bilderberg would be filled with one calamity after another. Even the Bilderberg itself would crumble—from her husband's actions, not her own—and she would be humiliated by the scandal.

Bernhard was the moving force behind the founding of Bilderberg, but he himself said the proposal first came from Dr. Joseph H. Retinger, who spent time in prison in the United States and was a champion of the Polish government-in-exile. Retinger was also an intelligence operative and staunch anti-Communist. He approached the man who was perhaps Bernhard's best friend, Dr. Paul Rijkens, and Rijkens persuaded Bernhard to become involved. The purpose of Bilderberg was to thrash out economic problems confronting and dividing Western nations and to coordinate efforts to stop the spread of communism. A number of European government and business figures agreed to attend, but it was understood the meeting would be fruitless without American participation. Bernhard contacted Walter Bedell Smith, then head of the CIA, and soon a large and important U.S. representation was assured.

Much of the agenda of the first meeting of Bilderberg was devoted to an airing of European fears about McCarthyism. It seemed to the Europeans that America was on the road to fascism, and they feared possible aggression aimed at them. C. D. Jackson, an interesting character, a close associate of Walter Bedell Smith and President Eisenhower's adviser on psychological warfare, spoke directly to the problem: "Whether McCarthy dies by an assassin's bullet or is eliminated in the normal American way of getting rid of boils on the body politic, I prophesy that by the time we hold our next meeting he will be gone from the American scene."

And he was.

Bilderberg meetings were often heated. In 1957 there was nearly a fistfight among representatives from the United States, France, and Great Britian over Suez, and at a later meeting there was strong disagreement about Quemoy and Matsu. Bilderberg almost immediately was viewed as sinister and undemocratic by people with both rightist and leftist leanings, and indeed much that was agreed on at meetings did become translated into public policy. The idea of the European Common Market was born at Bilderberg.

No wives were allowed to attend Bilderberg meetings, not even the Queen of the Netherlands. Juliana was busy with the necessary but less exciting matters of overseeing the government and raising her four children. Marijke was attending elementary school with twelve other boys and girls. "I wear glasses," she informed her teacher on the first day, "because, you see, my eyes are not very good."

The classroom Marijke attended was equipped with a special green blackboard that made seeing easier and was designed to be bright and airy. She demanded extra attention from her teacher, who finally told her there were other classmates who also needed help. "Strict here, isn't it?" said Marijke to one of her little friends.

Beatrix, on the other hand, was already a young woman in 1954. She wore chic gowns and expensive jewelry, but Juliana had no intention of letting her socialize with male friends. In this respect Juliana intended to be as strict as Wilhelmina. She figured she was raising another Queen.

Juliana herself was very informal. Often she would eat a light lunch and then make unannounced calls to schools, social institutions, and even neighboring housewives. Many Dutch women have been surprised to see Juliana's limousine pull up in front of their homes, and the Dutch people loved to read about it. Juliana would come dressed as any other drop-in neighbor, and although her unassuming manner and plain talk could not completely put her hosts at ease, they helped.

Juliana spoke flawless English, smoked American cigarettes, enjoyed her Martinis dry, and often spent her evenings watching motion pictures in the theater at Soestdijk Palace. When earlier, on the American trip in 1952, Juliana had visited Hollywood, she attended a party packed with motion picture stars. "Your faces all look so familiar to me!" she blurted out. "You have been in my home many times."

It was this naiveté and her lack of pretension that

endeared her to the people in Holland. In 1954 she ordered her chauffeur to pick up a policeman whose car had broken down. The cop asked if he could be taken to an accident that had occurred twenty kilometers ahead. He did not realize that the woman in the backseat was Queen Juliana, and when he was left off, he said, "Thank you very much. You have rendered a real service to your country."

Sympathy exists in Holland for a republican form of government and the abolition of constitutional monarchy, but not nearly enough to make it happen. Republican leader Hendrik Lankhorst was asked who would be President if the monarchy were replaced. He thought it over, shook his head, and said, "Juliana."

Late in 1954 Juliana was patron of the first major show of Dutch paintings held in the United States since 1909. The exhibition consisted of almost a hundred paintings from Holland's Golden Age by such masters as Steen, Hals, Vermeer, and Rembrandt and was seen at New York's Metropolitan Museum of Art, the Toledo (Ohio) Museum of Art, and the Art Gallery of Toronto.

On December 29, 1954, Juliana had what she considered a much more pleasant chore than granting independence to Indonesia. Juliana signed, for Holland, the new Charter for the Kingdom of the Netherlands, which was promoted as the establishment of "a new commonwealth" granting "self-government and independence" to the former colonies of Surinam and the Netherlands Antilles "within a new union of the Netherlands." What really had occurred was that these exploited colonies were rebelling and a compromise was needed to keep them from being completely lost. In reality, very little was given to the former colonies in the way of independence or self-government. They did not handle their own foreign affairs, nor could they have their own armed forces. Investments remained solidly in the hands of the Dutch.

Juliana, early in 1955, paid an official visit to Surinam and the Netherlands Antilles. Incredibly, despite Holland's long history as a colonial power, it was the first time one of its sovereigns had visited a Dutch territory. That had been a complaint of the Indonesians: although their natural wealth was mercilessly shipped back to Holland, no Dutch monarch thought enough of them even to come and take a look. But Juliana, to whom the people of Surinam and the Netherlands Antilles still owed allegiance, seemed different from what they imagined a ruler of the House of Orange would be. She was no strutting William III or cool, aloof Wilhelmina, and some formerly uncommitted people in the newly formed "Kingdom of the Netherlands" believed the arrangement might work. At Willemstad, in the Netherlands Antilles, she said: "We are attending a symbolical manifestation of your independence, which at the same time means a fully autonomous and equal partnership with Surinam and the Netherlands." Then, at Paramaribo, in Surinam: "You are part of the Kingdom of the Netherlands, which must henceforth be fully aware of the fact that it consists of three independent, equal, associated parts."

Subsequent events, however, would not justify Juliana's optimism. For one thing, a nation such as Holland that largely had justified its colonial holdings with inherently racist reasoning could not turn itself around so suddenly. Surinam, for example, on the northeastern coast of Latin America, had been a colony of the Netherlands since the seventeenth century. The Netherlands Antilles consists of six Caribbean islands: Aruba, Curaçao, Bonaire, St. Eustatius, Saba, and the southern part of St. Maarten (the northern part belongs to France). As J. E. Hartshorn pointed out in *Politics and World Oil Economics,* "The refineries of Shell at Curaçao and Esso at Aruba, processing Venezuelan oil, make these Dutch islands one of the most important export refining centres of the world." Although people in Surinam and the Netherlands Antilles now had the right to live in Holland because of the charter Juliana had signed, those who emigrated did not like what they found. "There is very decided discrimination on the labour market and in the housing sector," reported J. M. M. van Amserfoort in *Surinamese Immigrants in the Netherlands,* and a visitor to Holland needs only to talk with a cross section of society to discover how true the remark is. Perhaps it was not coincidental that the three largest Dutch corporations, Royal Dutch Shell, Philips, and Unilever—all among the top five industrial companies in the world outside the United States—had significant investments in South Africa. It has been estimated that Shell, in combination with British Petroleum, supplies about one-third of South Africa's oil requirements.

Juliana was happy to return to Holland after the official visits to the former colonies and settle back into the life with which she was most comfortable. She had no real hobbies, but she had begun to enjoy being Queen, and she was developing a deserved reputation for thrift. A Dutch journalist close to the royal court revealed how she would travel into neighboring towns to comparison-shop for items as inexpensive as a garden hose. It seemed almost humorous, this rich monarch trying to save pennies while surrounded by hundreds of servants, but it was not amusing at all to Bernhard. He, too, was learning that the Queen of the Netherlands was no spendthrift.

Bernhard had always been interested in hunting—he often enjoyed going out in the royal forests before breakfast and shooting a deer or a wild boar—but in 1955 it became a major hobby of his. That year he went on a safari to Tanganyika, hired twenty bearers, purchased expensive equipment, and shot three elephants, a lion, a buffalo, a rhinoceros, and numerous other animals. "He wanted a trophy of each species," wrote his trusted biographer Alden Hatch, "and as usual he was a young man in a hurry."

Actually, he was forty-four years old.

Bernhard continued to go on African safaris whenever he could get away from his many government and business commitments. He also took time to vacation in Iran, where he and the Shah hunted wild sheep together.

Princess Beatrix turned eighteen on January 31, 1956, and was confirmed as a member of the Dutch Reformed Church. She was given a yacht by the people of the Netherlands and was installed by Juliana as a member of the Council of State, a legally required action the Queen could not have enjoyed performing. Beatrix was now old enough to become monarch, and with the Greet Hofmans situation about to explode she was showing little reluctance to assume the position. In fact, she seemed eager to take over.

But Juliana had a good deal working for her. The Netherlands, after a slow postwar recovery complicated by the great 1953 flood and especially the loss of Indonesia, had entered a period of dynamic industrial expansion. The gross national product was rising at 4.5 percent a year and industrial production at more than 6 percent annually; the Dutch people were not looking for change. And particularly on a personal level Juliana had won many loyal supporters. It was good for her that she had, because not long after the government began hoping the Greet Hofmans episode had been an unfortunate but isolated incident, nothing more than a temporary aberration, Juliana shocked Dutch society with an even stranger performance.

11

*What Bernhard was doing was selling
invitations to Soestdijk Palace.*

Iᴛ ʜᴀᴘᴘᴇɴᴇᴅ on a sunny late May afternoon in 1959. Juliana's specially invited guest, who was holding forth at a press conference on the lawn of Soestdijk Palace, was a most unusual man. The Dutch cabinet, Bernhard, her advisers, members of her court, all had pleaded with Juliana not to see him, especially not in public and preferably not at all. But for Juliana it was a matter of great personal interest, and her conscience was also involved; in this latter respect she had never exhibited much of a tendency to back down.

Juliana's guest was George Adamski, age sixty-eight, medium height, a wiry, gray-haired former California hamburger stand operator who had founded a Temple of Scientific Philosophy in Laguna Beach. Adamski had also studied the teachings of Gurdjieff and believed in unusual methods of healing, even though he knew Gurdjieff's most publicized effort in that direction had ended in disaster. The Russian mystic advised the writer Katherine Mansfield, who had tuberculosis, to live in a cow barn so that she could breathe the "energized air"

exhaled by cows. Katherine Mansfield followed this advice and soon died, prompting her friends to blame
Gurdjieff.

But it was not his familiarity with the teachings of
Gurdjieff that motivated Juliana to receive Adamski, who
had been chauffeured to Soestdijk Palace in a royal
limousine, but his reputation as a "philosopher, teacher,
student and saucer researcher." He claimed he had re-
searched flying saucers firsthand.

Earlier Adamski had written a book, *Flying Saucers
Have Landed,* the title of which gave away the story. The
book sold 100,000 copies and put Adamski in great demand as a speaker. Juliana wanted to see him because she
long had been intrigued by the possibility of contact with
beings from outer space, a major tenet of Gurdjieff's
philosophy.

Juliana listened intently as Adamski was questioned by
General Heye Schaper, Chief of Staff of the Dutch air
force, and by journalists and medical and space experts.
Adamski's speech was sprinkled with "deses" and "doses"
straight out of the Capone era in Chicago as he fielded
questions from first one and then another of his skeptical
interrogators. Their job was to discredit the man from
California and convince the Queen that he should be
under investigation by the bunko squad, but Juliana
seemed entranced by what she heard. Bernhard, standing
in the background, tried to look inconspicuous.

Adamski revealed that he had first met spacemen from
Venus while on a picnic in an Arizona desert. They
simply dropped out of the sky and made friends. They
were small, intelligent men with long hair and high
domes. When this story was greeted with astonishment,
Adamski merely shrugged and said he was an honest man
relating a true story, and he was sorry he was not believed.

But it was quite clear that Juliana was not dismissing the possibility, and the questioners were in a delicate position: they did not want to enrage the Queen, but it seemed to them that Adamski was a preposterous individual and that Juliana would do herself and the Netherlands great harm if she did not disavow him.

"What language did they use?" Adamski was asked.

"They are above such things," he explained.

Adamski reported that flying saucers were often a mile long and shaped like a cigar. The United States, he said, was behind the Russians in space technology because American officials would not open their minds to receive advice from invisible space visitors who were eager to help. Spacemen were peaceful beings, he pointed out, although they would defend themselves if attacked, which was what happened when a Florida scoutmaster started hacking away at a spaceship with his machete. Adamski detailed how he had visited a planet that cannot be seen from earth because it is shielded by the moon.

Adamski told Juliana he had made seven space flights in all. On one of these he was picked up in a hotel lobby by a man from Venus and another from Saturn and taken on a long voyage in space. The group was accompanied by two beautiful women named Ilmuth and Kalna, and the chief food was a "colorless liquid." Still another incident involved a girl from California who fell in love with and eloped with a Venusian and was never heard from again.

"Are we the most ignorant people in the universe?" Adamski said he asked one of the spacemen.

"No, my son," was the reply, "your world is not the lowest in development."

Some of Holland's leading men of science were at Soestdijk Palace to try to discredit Adamski and to convey the impression that the Queen was at least dubious, but those watching Juliana could see she was fascinated. Adamski was a pleasant man, not in the least strident, and he refused to be drawn into discordant debates. Except for his gangsterish tone of voice, he seemed to her nothing more than a sincere, honest individual with amazing stories to relate.

Later, at a press conference attended only by newsmen, Adamski hinted that he soon would be visiting Queen Elizabeth and Prince Philip at Buckingham Palace (with almost the speed of one of Adamski's spaceships, a spokesman for the English royal family denied it). Adamski also showed film he said he had taken in outer space. The motion pictures were cloudy and consisted of vague, bloblike objects darting back and forth against a gray background. The reporters thought they could have been anything. But the question everyone wanted answered was, What did Adamski think of Queen Juliana? "The world," said Adamski, "would be better off if there were more people like her."

"What did Queen Juliana think of *you*?"

"She agreed," said Adamski, "that the time is not far off when everybody will know that Venusians are already holding high posts in important governments all over the world."

Could it be true? Juliana refused to comment. Did Juliana think she was from Venus? Adamski refused to comment.

But Cornelis Kolff of the Dutch Aeronautical Association, who had been present on the lawn of Soestdijk Palace, said, "The Queen showed an extraordinary interest in the whole affair."

Juliana refused to disavow Adamski and the Dutch press went wild. The Catholic *De Volkskrant* called

Adamski a "court jester" and said that "in the past the Dutch press has been blamed—probably rightly so—for keeping silent too long when figures moved into the royal court who could be supposed to radiate too hovering a spirit." Labor's *Het Vrije Volk* called Adamski's reception at Soestdijk Palace "A disgrace for our country."

Once again the Netherlands became the butt of countless foreign jokes, some good-natured, some not, but the people of Holland seemed not that disturbed. They loved Juliana, and if she was a bit "quaint"—a word often used—that was all right and even sort of fun.

George Adamski died from a heart attack in a Takoma Park, Maryland, sanitarium on April 23, 1965. Just a month before he had called a press conference to announce that "a large fleet of interplanetary space vehicles will converge soon on the nation's capital."

The Adamski visit to Soestdijk Palace engendered new talk about abdication and renewed old fears that Juliana might be heeding the advice of crackpots. It was historically provable that monarchs in the past had been insane—often nothing could be done about it—but such an arrangement just was not permissible in twentieth-century Europe. Juliana's mental stability was discussed in business, political, and intellectual circles, but clearly she was nothing more than eccentric, and in a very human way at that. Once more, without compromising her beliefs by denouncing Adamski, she endured through the political controversy. Much, much stiffer tests lay just ahead.

Again in 1959 the Dutch people were in no mood for change; if anything, even less so than in 1956, when there was rapid industrial expansion and a rising gross national product, but considerable poverty and unemployment. In 1959 wages were going up and adequate living standards were more general. Although refusal to vote in the Netherlands is punishable by fine, a phenomenal 95.6 percent—the highest percentage in Dutch history—of eligible voters cast a ballot in 1959, another indication that people thought the current system could be made to work.

If hopeful about the state of the economy in the eleventh year of Juliana's reign, the family-oriented Dutch were also pleased with her performance as a mother. Regardless whether these qualities were inherited, Beatrix, quick-witted, highly intelligent—although surely not with an IQ of 159, as Bernhard boasted—was impressing her instructors at the University of Leyden. She was ambitious and motivated and a skilled modeler with clay, as well as being a workmanlike painter. Irene was a talented horsewoman, Margriet was interested in theater, and Marijke, with an excellent ear for music, was perhaps most gifted of all. Many people in the Netherlands consider the royal family to be part of *their* family, so Juliana's performance as a mother was often being evaluated and rated.

Juliana involved herself in numerous social programs, in the process earning additional goodwill for the monarchy. In August 1959 she joined the Red Cross hospital ship *Henri Dunant* for a canal cruise to raise money for chronic invalids, an indisputably good cause. During World Refugee Year (1959–1960) she lent her name to a number of committees and met with many displaced persons. Her work in these areas was recognized with an honorary doctorate degree in social sciences from the University of Groningen.

Of course, many of the displaced persons came from the former colony of Indonesia, and even people from Surinam and the Netherlands Antilles who came to Holland seeking a better life might be called displaced persons. In any event, they were a major concern of the Dutch government and presented a problem Juliana could address. As a prominent editor in the Netherlands wryly remarked, "We Dutch have been all too willing to grant asylum to rich Jews fleeing from the Inquisition and devout Pilgrims escaped from England. But poor blacks from the South American jungle? That's another matter."

The situation would grow worse in the Netherlands. A terrorist group called the Viking Youth would be formed to "clean up" refugee neighborhoods. They dressed like the Hitler Youth and derived their name from a Nazi regiment. Most people in Holland, although not friendly toward the refugees, wanted nothing to do with a neo-Nazi gang of toughs.

Besides, there were other youth in the Netherlands. In 1960 students at the Franklin Roosevelt School in Amsterdam sent a petition to President Eisenhower asking him to release two American blacks—ages seven and nine—who had been jailed in North Carolina. The seven-year-old's "crime" was that he had been kissed on the cheek by a six-year-old white girl, and the nine-year-old's "offense" was that he had witnessed it. Eisenhower did intervene and the children were freed. Eleanor Roosevelt, Juliana's old friend, also contacted President Eisenhower in the children's behalf.

Each summer Juliana and the family spent a month at their Italian villa, the Happy Elephant, a fabulous residence on the Mediterranean that Bernhard had built. Bernhard's relationship with elephants was a curious one: he shot a good number of them, even had a stool made out of an elephant leg, but he also decided they needed protection.

Bernhard helped found, and became president of, the World Wildlife Fund, an organization whose express purpose was to save wild animals and their habitat. He became interested in conservation, he said, because each time he went on safari in Africa the number of wild animals he could hunt was drastically reduced: "Where once I saw thousands, I found only a few hundred, then a mere handful of even the most common animals." That he himself might be partially responsible for the reduction did not seem seriously to occur to him, but in 1961 he helped launch the World Wildlife Fund. It was an organization at which more than once Juliana would look askance.

Bernhard raised $10 million by forming the 1001 Club—he was the one—and persuading a thousand people to join by donating $10,000 each. "What Bernhard was doing," a prominent Dutch journalist explained, "was selling invitations to Soestdijk Palace. It was understood that the donor was welcome to stop by and visit the royal family."

This was hardly an arrangement which Juliana approved, no matter how much she was in favor of saving wild animals, since some of the "guests" were people with dubious backgrounds needing favors. But there may have been more to the World Wildlife Fund than Bernhard's desire to save endangered species. Although numerous dedicated conservationists undoubtedly work for the Fund, there have been allegations that it has served various Western nations as an intelligence-gathering apparatus in Africa.

Juliana, meanwhile, continued to place her own impress on monarchy, and it seemed absolutely in tune with the wishes of her subjects. She treated being Queen as a job, not as a super-elevated, distantly detached position of divine ordinance at which the people could stare up in awe. Juliana performed the boring, tedious ceremonial duties of a monarch without the trace of a complaint. She presented awards to artists, faithfully pored over voluminous documents that required her signature, was always available to boost morale in times of crisis, and made a favorable impression whenever she had to greet important state visitors. In 1961 she helped celebrate Bernhard's fiftieth birthday at a spectacular party where he was presented with an expensive cabin cruiser paid for with contributions from industry and labor. He named the cabin cruiser *Budi,* which is an elephant that has no tusks.

On July 7, 1961, Beatrix was awarded a law degree from the University of Leyden. Already she was receiving a state salary and serving in important government positions (most important, the Council of State), and soon she was celebrating her graduation aboard the ship the Dutch people had given her on her eighteenth birthday: the *Green Dragon.* Beatrix's graduation was cause for a family celebration. The University of Leyden was built by William the Silent as a gesture of thanks to the courageous people of the town. During the desperate war for independence against Spain, Leyden's Burgomaster had offered his own body to be eaten rather than allow the people to surrender because of hunger.

Juliana was approaching her twenty-fifth wedding anniversary in late 1961. Her marriage was described as "very shaky" and "barely hanging together" even by conservative publications, and it was a source of no happiness to her. That Bernhard had intimate relations with other women was now beyond doubt, and he seemed to operate with similar abandon in corporate and government affairs. Earlier Juliana might have sought advice from Wilhelmina, whose Prince Henry had seemed of a like bent, but the former Queen was eighty-one and dying. Some of the last words Wilhelmina wrote convey vividly the way she was thinking: "We must not forget to see the present as the road to what *will be one day,* to what was promised in the words 'He will be all in all.' To see the postponement of this day in the true Light of His Love and His patient waiting, in order to give to all until the very last a full chance of coming out of darkness into His miraculous Light. . . . Now I consider my duty accomplished, which was to show you how everything in my life was guided and had its significance in Christ's supreme plan."

Juliana's beliefs were similar, but try as she did she could not make the beliefs banish the specters that seemed to loom up ahead. If everything was guided by "Christ's supreme plan," why did her personal future look so dark? She did have hopes that the children, to whom she had given so much love, might make everything all right, but there were even disturbing indications in that regard. Juliana was almost fifty-three years old and it appeared that life might soon overwhelm her.

But first there were duties to perform, one of these being to host a gigantic party which, if not gay, would almost certainly be sensational.

12

Let us never forget to put ourselves in the children's position, as they have been placed in our world.

JULIANA IS RELATED in one way or another to every monarch in Europe and to almost every noble of any stature whatever. They all decided to come to Amsterdam on April 30, 1962, for the joint celebration of Juliana's fifty-third birthday and twenty-fifth wedding anniversary (the wedding anniversary was actually January 7). This "must" event on the social calendar turned into one of the century's most glittering displays of royalty: from England came Queen Elizabeth and Prince Philip; from Norway, King Olav V; from Belgium, King Baudouin and Queen Fabiola; Grand Duchess Charlotte, Prince Jean, and Prince Felix of Luxembourg; Princess Marina, the Duchess of Kent; Prince Karl von Hesse; the Shah of Iran and Empress Farah; and scores of lesser lights.

The Dutch government put up $28,000 to help finance the affair, an amount that would not even cover the food bill, but Juliana dipped into her own finances to pay other costs, such as housing and entertainment. Some 130 guests were lodged in Amsterdam's plush Amstel Hotel, and for celebrity watchers that establishment was paradise. But for the people of the Netherlands there was only one monarch: more than 1.5 million of them stood in the streets to shout *"Hiep! Hiep! Hoera!"* when Juliana's carriage came into view. Others burst into a patriotic song, "Tulips of Amsterdam, Offered to You, Our Queen." For royalty from other countries, Juliana's guests, there was only mild applause.

On the official agenda was a visit to the Keukenhof tulip fields, but getting there would be a problem because of traffic jams caused by people who had come to catch a glimpse of royalty, and others who were attending a European soccer cup final. Juliana delighted the people of the Netherlands by requisitioning three buses, but it was a solution that did not please everyone. Many of the guests had never ridden on a bus in their lives and wanted to keep that record intact. Others, however, seemed to relish the experience of "slumming" and praised Juliana for her ingenuity. Her abundant liquor supply made the experience less traumatic for everyone.

The extravagant party Juliana gave aboard the luxury liner *Oranje* was more pleasant for the royal guests. The ship cruised along the North Sea Canal, her bejeweled passengers drinking, dancing, and gossiping. Juliana, more like a schoolmistress than a Queen, started the dancing by clapping her hands. Gossip spread about twenty-four-year-old Beatrix, who was escorted by Bob Steensma, twenty-five, a lawyer. Was this extravagant affair also meant to introduce Steensma to royal society as Beatrix's future husband? At stake, everyone knew, was more than the marriage of a likely future Queen, but the marriage of an heiress to one of Europe's great fortunes, and none in this crowd was unaware of the importance of money.

There was also considerable speculation about Irene. She probably would never rule the Netherlands, but royal onlookers tried to identify each hopeful young prince who stood in the long line waiting to dance with her.

Because Juliana's two oldest daughters were old enough to marry, most of the gossip concerned them, but there was much more to talk about. Prince Philip, doing the twist, was a hit on the dance floor; Queen Elizabeth stuck to waltzes. The stunning Empress Farah was the most ogled. Even Baroness Armgard was much discussed. Armgard had converted to Catholicism, a not very controversial action except in the Netherlands, where some of the leading nobility are said still to be fighting William the Silent's war against Spain. Armgard, always the life of the party, seemed unconcerned by the gossip.

The *Oranje* did not dock until 4 A.M., and waiting limousines returned the bleary-eyed guests to the Amstel Hotel. The cruise, everyone agreed, had been a triumph for Juliana, but for Juliana herself it was merely a respite from the storm she knew was gathering. Nor could the people of the Netherlands have known what Juliana sensed as a certainty. They saw her present two youth centers, and a gift of her own money, to children in Holland, and she seemed as plain and stolid as ever, almost a "rock," as Wilhelmina had been.

Juliana delivered many speeches championing the rights of children, of which the following is typical:

Let us never forget to put ourselves in the children's position, as they have been placed in our world. They, the people of tomorrow, have no say in the disastrous happenings, the discords in the adult world, and they stand bewildered. They have a right to food and drink, to be healthy and to build up their own world in their play. It is they who have to build the adult world of the future. It is essential that they be given the chance to develop in body and mind as harmonious human beings. But most important of all, a child must be surrounded with love. No one can live without receiving love, or without feeling wanted for his own sake. In fact, no human being lives without giving love. To live is to live for someone else.

Not many rulers talk this way, and Juliana's seeming sincerity, combined with the debt the people of the Netherlands felt they owed her and the House of Orange, made it easy to understand why less than 10 percent of the population wanted to do away with the monarchy and establish a republic or some other form of government. Perhaps a Dutch shipyard worker put it best: "When the politicians are arguing and nothing can get done, Queen Juliana can step in and cut all the red tape. She can say, 'Do it!'"

The question, of course, is what the monarch will order to be done. Will it be good or bad? With Juliana the people had very little fear. She seemed to serve more as an ombudsman, an impartial arbiter of disputes, than a queen: she blocked a landlord from evicting a tenant family; she stopped the expulsion of illegal immigrants, a mother and her three children; she harassed the bureaucracy, which feared her anyway, into delivering pension checks on time. If she also profited when Royal Dutch Shell raised the price of gasoline for Dutch motorists, or lent support to some brutal dictator by visiting his country, or ordered police out against a strike, these events were overlooked.

It helped in 1962 that the economy of the Netherlands was continuing to surge upward. That year, as Frank Huggett pointed out in *The Modern Netherlands,* "the country had an enormous stroke of good luck, when large deposits of natural gas were found at Slochteren in the northern province of Groningen. It transpired to be one of the biggest fields in the world with known reserves of 1,650,000 million cubic metres. The state has a direct share in the exploitation of the gas, which was discovered by a subsidiary of Royal Dutch Shell and Esso."

At this time Juliana's mixed feelings about Beatrix were chief among her concerns. Juliana had done her best, even given special attention to her oldest daughter, because she was likely to succeed to the throne, but she feared it had not been enough. Beatrix was impatient, willful, almost arrogant. The bright, precocious Princess showed no reluctance to second-guess her mother—she still began sentences, "When I'm the Queen . . ."—or sneer at her odd religious beliefs, but Juliana felt duty-bound to prepare her as the heir of the House of Orange, and she gave all the support she could. In 1962 Beatrix traveled extensively in Europe, called on the Netherlands Antilles and Surinam, then journeyed to the oil-rich Middle East and to Japan. All was part and parcel of the education a monarch would need. Beatrix was called back from Japan to the Netherlands on November 28, 1962, for the funeral of her grandmother, Wilhelmina. Juliana lost her most trusted religious confidante, and her best friend too, when Wilhelmina died. It was a magnificent white funeral— Juliana sobbing—attended by representatives of every European state. A giant had died.

If Bernhard had been prone to bullying to achieve his ends, or if politicians and businessmen clamored for her abdication, she could count on Wilhelmina for support and strength. Now it would be necessary to manage on her own.

She did fairly well in 1963. There were state visits to Iran and Thailand, and Juliana, fifteen years on the throne, still captured the hearts of people with her plain, retiring manner. But serious trouble was brewing, and from an unlikely source: Princess Irene.

Irene had converted to Catholicism in the summer of

Juliana with her parents, Queen Wilhelmina and Prince Henry of Mecklenburg-Schwerin, in 1920. (Wide World Photos)

Above: *Juliana as a young girl.*
(The Bettmann Archive, Inc.)
Right: *Queen Wilhelmina in*
1947. (Wide World Photos)

Right: *Princess Juliana and Prince Bernhard vacationing in the Alps. (Culver Pictures)*
Below: *The wedding of Princess Juliana and Prince Bernhard zu Lippe-Biesterfeld.*
(The Bettmann Archive, Inc.)

Juliana and Prince Bernhard with their daughter Princess Beatrix at the age of four months. (Culver Pictures)

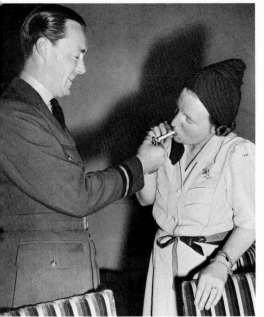

Left: *Prince Bernhard and Crown Princess Juliana at the Netherlands Club in 1942. The Prince later told a crowd of three thousand that "there is unity of the people of Holland" in their "brave resistance against their aggressor." (Culver Pictures)*

Below: *Queen Juliana and Prince Consort Bernhard on the throne dais in the Nieuwe Kirk in Amsterdam at Juliana's investiture as Queen of the Netherlands in 1948. (Wide World Photos)*

Above: *Dutch faith healer
Greet Hofmans.
(Wide World Photos)*
Right: *In May 1959, George
Adamski, an American who
claimed to have made trips into
outer space, was the guest of
Queen Juliana at the royal
palace at Soestdijk.
(Wide World Photos)*

The Dutch royal family in 1964 (left to right): Princess Margriet, Queen Juliana, Prince Bernhard, Princess Marijke (also known as Christina), and Princess Beatrix. (UPI Color Photo)

Aerial view of Soestdijk, the royal palace, showing the festivities held in honor of Queen Juliana's sixty-seventh birthday. (Nationaal Fotopersburo)

Queen Juliana and Prince Bernhard wave to well-wishers from the steps of the royal palace on April 30, 1976, Juliana's sixty-seventh birthday. (United Press International)

1963, but for months the Dutch people were not told. Irene had studied at the University of Utrecht, then went to Spain to learn its language. The first news that she was Catholic was conveyed in a photograph showing her kneeling at mass in the Royal Church of Jeronimo in Madrid. Immediately there was suspicion she was engaged to a Catholic, and the suspicion was correct: he was Prince Carlos Hugo of Bourbon Parma, thirty-three years old and a claimant to the Spanish throne. It would have been almost impossible to select a more unfavorable marriage partner than Carlos Hugo.

Juliana immediately tried to head off the wedding. It was disastrous politically. The Dutch people, encouraged by Holland's powerful nobility, had never forgiven Spain for its high-handed treatment of the Netherlands, and in addition they detested Franco for his support of the Nazis. Prince Carlos Hugo was a political ally of Franco and a leader in the Falange (fascist) Party of Spain. *Time* magazine explained Carlos Hugo's claim to the throne: "A split in the Spanish royal family happened in 1833 when King Ferdinand VII died without a son, after changing the law of succession so that his daughter Isabella Maria II could follow him. Ferdinand's younger brother Don Carlos refused to recognize Isabella's right to the throne and led an unsuccessful rebellion; descended from him is a list of chronically unsuccessful Carlist pretenders, including Irene's fiancé."

Juliana posthaste dispatched a private secretary to Madrid to dissuade Irene. It was inconceivable to Juliana that her daughter would guarantee the anger of the Dutch people by marrying a fascist, someone whose tenuous claim to the throne of Spain was supported only by the most reactionary Spanish nobility. The secretary informed Juliana that the engagement was canceled, that Irene had come to her senses and would fly home. But when the airplane arrived, Irene was not on it.

The Dutch people waited impatiently for news. At this time there was a rare unanimity among all classes of Holland's society: the richest nobles, fearing a Catholic influence, and the most humble worker, remembering the Nazis, were joined in opposition to the proposed marriage. Finally Juliana, not knowing the true status of the engagement, agreed to speak on nationwide radio. She was heartsick and refused to appear on television for fear of breaking down. Yet it was a blunder to go on radio and say what she did: "Alas, our daughter Irene has informed us that this engagement will not take place. Our daughter is now passing an extremely difficult time." But in reality the blonde, buxom Irene was suffering very little compared to what her mother was going through. There was evidence that the engagement was not off, that Irene had changed her mind again after talking to the private secretary, and angry people throughout the Netherlands— this time a significant cross section of average citizens— talked about being betrayed and that perhaps it would be best if Juliana abdicated. How, they wondered, could Juliana raise a daughter so totally insensitive to the wishes of her people. This response by her constituency was proof to Juliana that she had been right in her conception of modern monarchy surviving only so long as it was responsive to specific needs of subjects. In the past, even though faced with hostility from the business establishment and the nobility that preferred Beatrix, Juliana could count on the support of the nation's rank and file. But now even this seemed to be slipping away.

Juliana and Bernhard climbed aboard a military plane for a flight to Spain. Surely, Juliana believed, Irene would listen to reason. But on a stopover in Paris, Juliana received an urgent communiqué from the Dutch government saying it would resign en masse if she continued on to Spain, a country no ruling member of the House of Orange had ever visited. Juliana returned to the Netherlands in tears.

Irene went into hiding. First she stayed in a Catalonian convent, then she moved into a suite of rooms near Carlos Hugo. The two communicated by standing at windows and exchanging hand signals. Both were afraid their telephones were tapped, both suspected Irene might be kidnapped and taken back to the Netherlands. The stakes were high, and while neither could believe Juliana would be involved in such intrigue, there were powers close to the Dutch court that might do anything to protect the Queen.

Spanish dictator Francisco Franco inserted himself into the scene. He went out of his way to receive Carlos Hugo, fueling speculation that he might choose him as his successor rather than the current favorite, Don Juan. A marriage into the House of Orange, Franco may have figured, would increase Spain's prestige, an idea that may not have eluded Carlos Hugo either. Also, such a marriage might enhance Spain's chances for fuller economic partnership with other European nations. On Irene's part, it seemed unlikely she would ever assume the Dutch throne, what with Beatrix ahead of her, but possibly her husband could rule in Spain.

Religious antagonisms were inflamed by the situation. The Dutch Reformed Church wrote to Bernhard Jan Cardinal Alfrink, Archbishop of Utrecht, saying it "was most shocked by the fact that her conversion was not immediately made public by you" and asking "for clarification of the matter in the interests of ecumenical understanding." Cardinal Alfrink replied that Irene's activities within the Catholic Church were in the same category as "secrets of the confessional."

Early in February 1964 Irene said she was ready to come home. Bernhard flew to Madrid—the Dutch government still would not consider allowing the monarch to go—and returned to the Netherlands with both Irene and Carlos Hugo. The three were then whisked to Soestdijk Palace for six hours of heated debate with Juliana, Prime Minister Marijnen, and three senior ministers.

Carlos Hugo, who had attended Oxford and the Sorbonne, had different expectations than Juliana. He started by demanding a huge Roman Catholic wedding in Amsterdam's Protestant Nieuwe Kerk and saying he expected all of Europe's royalty to attend. Juliana explained that she wanted no wedding at all, that Irene's marriage to someone with Carlos Hugo's credentials could bring down the House of Orange, and this she had no intention of allowing to happen. Clearly neither side was going to compromise, so Prime Minister Marijnen laid it on the line: in order for Irene to maintain her right of succession to the Dutch throne, she needed approval for her marriage from the States-General, and given the mood of the country, there was no chance it would be granted. Irene thereupon did renounce her right of succession.

Considerable sympathy began building up for Irene in the Netherlands. She portrayed herself as being persecuted for her religious beliefs, even went so far as to declare that one reason she was marrying Carlos Hugo was to help bring about an end to religious intolerance. Irene's argument had appeal in a country more than 40 percent Catholic which had been governed by the Protestant House of Orange since the time of William the Silent. Additionally, there was sympathy for a young woman who seemed so in love that she was willing to denounce her precious right of succession. Many in the Netherlands believed Irene was being unjustly treated, but there were others, more skeptical, who could not forget Carlos Hugo's politics and ambition.

Juliana wondered where she had gone off the track. She had always been a mother first, the Queen second, but when she said, "You can't do such a thing to me," to Irene, her daughter brushed the remark aside. What many observers believe happened was that Juliana had allowed her daughters just enough freedom to lose control over them, but not enough to permit them always to exercise the best judgment. No one thought for a moment that if Wilhelmina were still alive and at the height of her powers the marriage would even be talked about.

Juliana continued to work behind the scenes to try to stop the upcoming wedding, making sure all lines of communication were kept open, but her efforts were sabotaged when Irene and Carlos Hugo had an audience in Rome with Pope Paul VI. The meeting was supposed to be kept secret, but a photograph leaked out. It was another moment of deep embarrassment for Juliana. At the same time her aides were denying the story, Wirephotos arrived at Dutch newspaper offices. Speculation was rampant about the Netherlands' being used in a "Franco-papal plot."

Irene and Carlos Hugo flew to Amsterdam after the meeting with Pope Paul VI, and Juliana pleaded one last time to stop the marriage. Unbelievably, Carlos Hugo once again talked about a big wedding at Nieuwe Kerk attended by Europe's crowned heads of state. Juliana told him it was impossible and warned Irene that members of the Dutch royal family would not attend the wedding no matter where it was held.

Shortly after this unpleasant family argument, Irene was scheduled to accompany Juliana on an official state visit to Mexico. What occurred was a sad, humiliating experience for Juliana. With numerous reporters looking on, she waited at Schiphol Airport for Irene to show up, but there was no sign of her daughter. She delayed the departure of the airplane, but still no Irene. Shaken, shoulders slumped, she boarded the plane to go to Mexico and do her duty.

Irene, retaliating because Juliana refused to sanction the marriage, announced publicly that she supported Carlos Hugo's claim to the Spanish throne *and* his Falangist politics. The statement promptly lost for Irene whatever goodwill she had built by championing an end to religious prejudice. When she was photographed attending a Falange rally in Spain, most Dutch citizens agreed it was just as well she had promised to live outside the country.

Irene and Carlos Hugo were married in Rome on April 29, 1964, one day before Juliana's fifty-fifth birthday, by the former papal internuncio to The Hague. No important members of royalty attended, chiefly out of a desire not to offend Juliana, and of course none of Irene's family was present.

The engagement and subsequent marriage of Irene and Carlos Hugo unleashed a storm of hostility that was directed against Juliana from every level of Dutch society. She was the monarch, the good Queen and mother, and the people of the Netherlands felt betrayed and blamed her. Most respected among the critics were members of the World War II Resistance, who had risked their lives in the fight against fascism and now were not about to suppress their anger and disbelief that such a wedding could even be contemplated. The privileged nobility was disturbed because the marriage, had it been approved by the States-General, would have overturned the long-standing tradition of Protestant rule in the Netherlands (nothing in the Dutch Constitution excludes a Catholic from reigning). Intellectuals were upset because the affair demonstrated serious insensitivity on the part of at least one member of the House of Orange, a ruling family they had persuaded themselves was attuned to progressive thought. But by far the most important was the vast majority of the Dutch people, who had witnessed fascism firsthand and wanted nothing to do with it.

Juliana had not helped her own cause early on by hosting her daughter's future in-laws—Carlos Hugo's parents, Prince Xavier and Princess Magdalena—and by not acting firmly against the marriage until it was clear that Dutch public opinion was opposed to it. On the other hand, while Juliana took the blame, it was forgotten that Holland's Cabinet had toasted Irene and Carlos Hugo with champagne and talked about a gala May wedding in Utrecht before the groom's political affiliations become general knowledge. It was this same Cabinet that threatened to resign when Juliana wanted to travel to Spain to dissuade Irene.

Juliana had also seemed indecisive during the crisis, a quality not admired in monarchs. Also, she appeared to have lost control over events. She had announced on nationwide radio that Irene's engagement was off when it was not. She gave permission to aides to declare Irene had not met with Pope Paul VI when she had. She stood in an airport, watched by reporters, waiting for a daughter who was lost. Most important of all, despite Juliana's power and wealth, she could not in the end stop the marriage. This latter was probably the most unfair of the allegations. The determined Irene was of age. What could Juliana have done?

Juliana was left puzzled and hurt and really did not understand the firestorm of protest. She thought she had been in touch with the deepest feelings of the Dutch people; no one could deny she had visited, and listened, in the most humble homes, and she had always been generous with her time whenever crises arose, even minor ones. And when her subjects said no to the marriage, she opposed it too. Juliana wished she could talk with Bernhard, but they had grown apart and he was away much of the time, or with Wilhelmina, but she had died. So she retreated further and further into prayer.

The threat to Juliana's throne had been very serious. The reality that the Netherlands has a Queen does not imply the country is undemocratic: Holland has *proportional* representation, which means that even tiny parties have a voice in the States-General, how many voices being dependent on the number of votes a party receives. By most reckonings the Netherlands is more democratic than the United States. In the United States there are Democrats and Republicans and very little else. In the Netherlands as many as fifteen parties have representation in the legislative body. Not many of these supported the Irene–Carlos Hugo marriage.

Juliana lasted out still another threat to her reign because the wedding took place outside the Netherlands, no member of the House of Orange attended it, and she had a reservoir of allegiance that could still be drawn from. Also, Irene was not the heiress presumptive, Beatrix was, and it was Beatrix the people of the Netherlands assumed Juliana had groomed to rule.

Citizens in Holland still shake their heads, saddened and amazed, when they recall the day Beatrix was married.

13

*I could be married in The Hague or
Rotterdam and win over either city. But if
I win the hearts of the Amsterdamers, I will
win the heart of all the Netherlands.*

Eₐᵣₗy ɪɴ ᴊᴜʟy 1965 Juliana appeared on nationwide radio and television to announce the engagement of twenty-seven-year-old Beatrix to Claus-Georg Wilhelm Otto Friedrich Gerd von Amsberg, thirty-eight, a West German diplomat who had held several posts in Africa. "I assure you," said Juliana, speaking from Soestdijk Palace, "it is a good thing."

The Dutch people did not think so. Claus von Amsberg had worn the hated uniform of the Nazi Wehrmacht and been a member of the Hitler Youth. It seemed absolutely incredible to most people in the Netherlands that Juliana would permit such a marriage, especially after the Irene–Carlos Hugo affair. And Beatrix's engagement was much more significant: she was, as *Newsweek* pointed out, "heiress to a $950 million fortune" and next in line for the Dutch throne.

Soon there were demonstrations in the streets. Angry crowds chanted *"Claus raus! Claus raus! Claus raus!"*— "Claus get out." There were marches, rallies, demonstrations. Orange swastikas appeared all over the Netherlands;

somehow a protester got through security and swabbed a large orange swastika on the royal palace in Amsterdam. This was unusual behavior for the Netherlands, up until this time considered one of the most sedate European countries. Even strikes had been relatively rare, and the nation was considered extremely favorable territory for corporations.

Much of the nation sympathized with the demonstrations and began to wonder if there was a conscious pattern to the royal marriages: Wilhelmina married a right-wing playboy who begged for money from Hitler; Juliana married an SS man; Irene married an admitted fascist; and now Beatrix, the heiress presumptive, was engaged to a former member of the Hitler Youth. The House of Orange began to seem to some people like some medieval reincarnation that considered itself accountable to no one. In reality, the good-hearted Juliana was opposed to the marriage, but since she felt she could not stop it, she did not believe she should speak and cause even more controversy. In any case, no more did people in the Netherlands talk about abdication—Beatrix would succeed to the throne in that event—but the cry increasingly heard in the country was "Up the Republic!" Maybe, the worried Dutch people were beginning to think, they could do without a monarchy.

Still, the people of the Netherlands were slow to demand change. In February 1964 the Netherlands Institute for Public Opinion found that 86 percent wanted the monarchy retained. The figure dropped to 74 percent when Beatrix's engagement was announced by Juliana, but what probably did not register was that the support of those saying they were in favor of the Crown was not as firm as it once had been.

The Beatrix-Claus engagement struck some Dutch citizens as a betrayal of the loyalty they had always given the

House of Orange. During the German occupation, the Nazis had made it a criminal act to wear orange colors or a white carnation, Bernhard's symbol, yet on August 31, 1940, Wilhelmina's birthday, the Dutch flag flew proudly on several public buildings, and people cheered when RAF planes flew over the country dropping orange confetti and anti-Nazi pamphlets. The engagement also seemed insulting to that minority of the Dutch population about whom one Nazi officer sneered, "Tying up so many freight trains was the greatest blow the Jews dealt to Germany."

Even the Dutch press, mostly pro-royalist, was deeply disturbed by the proposed marriage. The 1960s were hardly the heyday of monarchy, and royal insensitivity could bring it all tumbling down. "Can a German," asked Rotterdam's *Nieuwe Courant,* "put flowers at our memorials for heroes he fought against?" Another publication offered a solution. Irene had given up her right to succeed to the Dutch throne, and the literary monthly *De Gide* suggested Beatrix should do the same. This would have placed Margriet next in line after Juliana, a thought that dried the throat of the ambitious Beatrix.

The press was joined in the chorus of complaints by prominent Dutch citizens, although one member of the States-General, a fan of English royalty, thought the engagement was just fine: "Sometimes," he said admiringly, "it looks as though Beatrix may have picked up a few ideas from Britain's Princess Margaret." More significant, six of Holland's most courageous and honored Resistance fighters issued a statement calling the upcoming marriage "unbearable." These were not radicals, looking for a political overturn, but plain, brave Dutch working people who had supported Wilhelmina during the war and felt the House of Orange had flirted long enough with the German right wing.

Some postwar German tourists in the Netherlands had not helped in smoothing the way for Claus von Amsberg. Some of these would go to Dutch beaches to sun themselves, wall off a portion with sand, and post an incredible sign reading "BESETZT," which means "OCCUPIED." Others would visit a Dutch home and ask if they could look inside because they had once lived there!

Much of the criticism was heaped on Juliana, who seemed to more than a few Dutch citizens to have perpetrated a hoax by appearing as the good mother and champion of children. In truth, she possessed those qualities, but her profound religious beliefs separated her from her "more modern" children and, just as in the case of Irene, she did not have Wilhelmina's steel constitution, which would have enabled her to enforce her ideas. To Beatrix, Juliana had always seemed vague, vacillating, off in her own world, someone who could be easily overcome. Certainly Juliana was weak where Bernhard was concerned: only when money was involved did she exercise any control over her husband. This was not, as Claus would learn, the sort of woman Beatrix intended to be. Claus, ambitious himself, perhaps came to wonder whether the prize was worth the effort.

Juliana had tried to prevent the marriage, an important fact most people in the Netherlands did not know. She had contacted the Foreign Minister in Bonn, von Amsberg's superior, and asked him to transfer Claus, who at the time was posted in Bonn, out of Europe. A request from such a rich and powerful individual—a head of state—could not be ignored, and Claus was about to be moved when Beatrix got wind of the scheme. Protesting, she went on a three-day royal hunger strike, and the worried Juliana gave in. "Juliana should have let Beatrix starve a little longer" was one opinion voiced in the Netherlands.

Juliana's appearance at this time was not that of a strong woman. She was fifty-six years old, and although physically she was healthy enough, she had put on weight and her eyes were tired. She still resembled a kindly matron, but the spring was gone from her step and her facial expression was often quizzical, confused.

Wilhelmina's autobiography was titled *Lonely but Not Alone,* yet the vulnerable Juliana was both lonely *and* alone. Her heart sank when she thought of Bernhard. He was allegedly seeing a beautiful woman who came to be known as "Paris Poupette," Helene Grinda, who reportedly soon gave birth to his child, Alexia. It was this relationship, Dutch journalists Willem Oltmans and Wim Klinkenburg believe, that ultimately helped lead to Bernhard's downfall. The effect, however, was to isolate Juliana, and alone she did not know how to stem the angry tide that was building in the country.

Juliana arranged for Beatrix and Claus von Amsberg to appear at a press conference and answer questions from journalists, and the result was a media success. The slim, smiling, handsome Claus could not have seemed less like a goose-stepping, order-obeying Nazi. He was a cheerful, modest, well-groomed man of medium height who seemed to answer questions openly and honestly. He quietly explained that he was in love with Beatrix, that he was sorry about his past, and that his most fervent wish was for acceptance by the Dutch people. Claus was mild and disarming, sincere. He discussed his experiences at the University of Hamburg, how he had come to meet Beatrix on a Swiss skiing vacation, why he hoped he could present the Netherlands with a male heir. Meeting the press was a small enough gesture, but in the Netherlands it was still a rare concession for the royal family to make, and some moderate elements in the country seemed willing to forgive Claus's past and give the marriage a chance.

Beatrix helped the situation when she was asked what she thought about the protesters. "It is much healthier," she said, "for people to speak their minds than to bottle up their feelings." It also helped when the government announced that it had checked with East Germany and the Soviet Union to see if there were any charges outstanding against Claus, and none existed. It looked as though the wedding, despite all odds, might come off smoothly.

But then Beatrix dropped another bombshell. She announced that the marriage would be held in Amsterdam, which had a liberal reputation and was the city that had suffered most from the Nazi occupation. "I could be married in The Hague or Rotterdam," she said, "and win over either city. But if I win the hearts of the Amsterdamers, I will win the heart of all the Netherlands." This declaration was doubtful at best. Almost 90 percent of Rotterdam had been flattened in the first few minutes of German bombing, and people in The Hague had suffered dearly also. But there were other reasons people in the Netherlands did not believe the reason Beatrix gave for wanting the wedding in Amsterdam. It seemed to them she was trying to demonstrate the lack of control public opinion had over her, that she was royalty and accountable to no one. Also, her explanation ignored Dutch tradition, which called for the monarch to be married at The Hague, inaugurated in Amsterdam, and buried at Delft. Juliana was opposed to Beatrix's plans for an Amsterdam wedding, but her daughter insisted on going ahead.

The States-General still had to approve the marriage if Beatrix was to remain in line for the throne, and the debate was carried on national television. It was a telecast watched by most of the nation. One legislator said he felt sorry for Claus, that he seemed a decent enough person, but he should be disqualified for the same reason a crippled person could not take part in professional sports. Such was the power of the House of Orange, however, that the November 1965 vote in the States-General was 132 to 9 in Beatrix's favor. This hardly ended the furor: anger was directed at the legislature, which seemed to some to be unresponsive to the will of the electorate.

Earlier, protesters had thrown anti-monarchist pamphlets into the ship that carried Beatrix and Claus on a tour of Amsterdam's beautiful canals. Now the agitation was stepped up, particularly in the wedding city, where 130,000 had been murdered by the German occupiers. Juliana was hurt and worried by the protests, which increasingly threatened to turn violent, and there was a further erosion of popular support for the monarchy: a Gallup poll showed that 71 percent of the Dutch people wanted to retain the throne for their country, a high percentage for most nations but almost an all-time low for the Netherlands.

The Dutch people were getting their point across in other ways besides protests in the streets. Juliana had been deluged by literally thousands of gifts on her wedding day, but a determined nationwide drive to raise $350,000 for a present for Beatrix produced less than $20,000. Driving home their point a few days later, in just twenty-four hours the Dutch contributed $350,000 to Indian famine relief. Even the pleasant, smiling, unobtrusive Claus could not soften the public's hostility. His mother began receiving letters signed, "with hate."

There seldom has been such a wedding day in the long annals of royal marriages. It began early in the morning with a large, angry march on the royal palace. Many of the demonstrators wore six-pointed Jewish stars, and soon they were fighting in the street with police. Tear gas clouded the air, nightsticks dented young heads; the protesters smashed windows and destroyed automobiles as they were beaten back. There were several arrests, but the bizarre day had just begun.

Later that same morning—March 10, 1966—Beatrix and Claus rode out from the royal palace in the golden coach. Both were smiling bravely, but they had been warned that there would be trouble.

Out of the crowd lining the street came a smoke bomb that rolled directly underneath the carriage and exploded. The royal couple completely vanished from view as the smoke billowed upward and police waded into the crowd swinging their batons with abandon. A number of innocent bystanders were clubbed to the ground. There was more fighting, more arrests; more bombs, smoke and stink alike, were thrown at the wedding procession. The sight of Beatrix and Claus seemed to charge the demonstrators with fury.

A dead chicken, a swastika painted on its body, thumped against the door of the golden coach. People who had just come to see the procession did not know whether to be more shocked by the demonstrators or by the police, who seemed to have lost control of themselves. Beatrix attempted to smile and wave, but smoke was burning her eyes and it appeared more likely she would cry. The eight footmen, all of them wearing bulletproof vests, moved closer to the besieged carriage.

More stink bombs and smoke bombs came hurtling from either side of the street. Gray columns of smoke rose more than fifty feet in the air. Juliana, witnessing the chaos and violence, sadly remembered how different her own wedding day had been, with the "100,000 Dutch girls" and more than a million other people cheering and wishing her well, but that had been before the war and the bitter experience of the occupation. On this day there was the very real possibility that her daughter Beatrix would be injured.

The day was different in other respects also. When Juliana was married, a glittering collection of royalty showed up. There was almost no one of note for this wedding. Most of Europe's nobility had invented an excuse not to attend, although the most important were all related to Juliana. They traced their roots back to a single source: Frederick V of Bohemia and his wife, Elizabeth. Frederick V was a grandson of William the Silent and his wife was the daughter of James I of England. One of their grandsons became King George I of England, and his son George II had a daughter who married Frederick V of Denmark. Another daughter of George II married Juliana's ancestor, William IV. Other descendants of the "Winter King," Frederick V, include the current monarchs of Sweden, Norway, and Belgium.

But reigning monarchs were not the only people avoiding Beatrix's marriage. Rabbis in the Netherlands were boycotting the affair, as were twenty-one members of Amsterdam's city council, and numerous local and national government employees.

"Claus raus!" was the cry heard most often in the streets, and people watching the royal procession were almost uniformly cool to it. A few unenthusiastic cheers for Beatrix and Claus were drowned out by noisy cries of "Up the Republic!"

The overzealous police did not cool tempers down. Later, in a separate incident, there would be considerable anger when it was learned they had arrested a young woman for passing out raisins and stripped her naked to search her. Eventually the Burgomaster of Amsterdam and the chief of police lost their jobs, such was the outcry over the beating of bystanders and the treatment of the woman.

The civil service was held in City Hall, and the religious ceremony at Westerkerk, the latter being another unfortunate choice. Westerkerk is just around the corner from 263 Prinsengracht, where Anne Frank lived, wrote, and hid until the day she was dragged away to the prison camps. The pathetic markings where she measured her height can still be seen in the house, now a museum, where she wrote the book that later was translated into more than forty languages. Incredibly, the police had wanted to use the house as their headquarters on the wedding day, but were told it would be closed.

Back at the royal palace, Beatrix and Claus made the traditional appearance on a tulip-bedecked balcony to receive the acclaim of the Dutch people. Fewer than two thousand were below to cheer the royal couple. It was the final humiliation of a humiliating day, a day Juliana would always recall with regret. Perhaps *Newsweek* best expressed what the people of Holland were thinking: "Unless Princess Beatrix develops a greater regard for the wishes of the people of her country, she may well wind up as the last member of the House of Orange to reign over the Netherlands."

As soon as the marriage was official, Claus became a Prince of the Netherlands and began drawing an $84,000 annual salary. But the protests that greeted the marriage flared once again nine days later when the police unwisely showed a photographic exhibit of their handling of the wedding riots. Demonstrators again took to the streets, clashing with police, inflicting damage to property, and setting fires in front of Dam Palace.

Although the Beatrix-Claus marriage produced the greatest outcry against monarchy in the Netherlands since P. J. Troelstra's attempted socialist takeover in 1918,

Juliana herself was not personally threatened as she had been with the Greet Hofmans episode, the George Adamski visit, or Irene's marriage to Carlos Hugo. Each of these incidents prompted demands that she abdicate in favor of Beatrix, something no one was calling for after the marriage to Claus. Each incident had been personally painful, especially for a monarch who had tried so hard to embody her people's best virtues, but the only danger for Juliana after Beatrix's marriage was that sentiment in the Netherlands might increase for the abolition of monarchy altogether. The government partly quelled her fears in this regard in the summer of 1966 by making her the highest-paid crowned head in Europe:

1.	Juliana of the Netherlands	$1,436,000
2.	Elizabeth II of England	$1,330,000
3.	Baudouin of Belgium	$1,068,000
4.	Frederick IX of Denmark	$657,000
5.	Gustav VI Adolf of Sweden	$533,000
6.	Constantine of Greece	$500,000
7.	Olav V of Norway	$225,000

There has never been much outcry in the Netherlands about the large amounts of money paid to the royal family and spent on the royal residences, even though Juliana has her own great private fortune. People in England seem much more willing to complain about Elizabeth's Civil List. "Most of us," said a worker from The Hague, "would be willing to give Queen Juliana much more."

Juliana's popularity, even when it slumps at times like that of the Beatrix-Claus marriage, unquestionably is higher than that of any politician in the Netherlands, or any politician almost anywhere else also. The reasons can be found in the unusual ways the people of the Netherlands have found to identify with her.

14

*The people have faith that their future
is safely entrusted to Queen Juliana.*

THE DUTCH PEOPLE pay large amounts of money to
support Juliana and the royal family, and a question often
asked by those outside the country is why. Several theories
exist. One holds that people are automatically attracted
to someone with prestige, and Juliana, with her money
and power, certainly possesses plenty of prestige. Another
theory, as Percy Black pointed out in *The Mystique of
Modern Monarchy,* contends that "self-abnegation before
greatness is traceable to the fearful cringing and death-
feigning of our pre-human ancestors in the presence of
superior might." Still another theory proposes that a
monarch enables a nation to envision its own history,
greatness, and potential by concentrating on a single
powerful individual.

Most U.S. and French citizens project little enthusiasm
for the idea of monarchy. America overthrew a monarch,
and the French beheaded theirs. Nevertheless, the fascina-
tion of monarchy persists even for these people. For instance, during Queen Elizabeth's coronation, millions of
Americans stayed home to watch the spectacular on tele-

vision, and Paris sidewalks were clogged with French citizens watching TV through store windows.

Many people in the Netherlands who catch a glimpse of Juliana, even at a distance, talk about it for weeks and months. The mere sight of her attaches glamour to their lives, and seeing her close up is cause for celebration. These actions are consciously encouraged by lavish royal displays of pomp and ceremony—people love a parade— which serve as colorful diversions from the gray business of everyday living. The master himself, Machiavelli, remarked that a prince who wanted to remain in power had better not neglect the pageantry of royalty. A British businessman, talking about Queen Elizabeth, put it differently: "We pay her a great deal, and the least we expect is a good show for the money."

Juliana recognized early on the need to maintain certain ceremonial aspects of monarchy. She cut down on the amount of curtsying—she had no need to salve her ego with false or servile displays—but she did not altogether eliminate it. When a group of college students visited her, she insisted that each person address her as "Your Royal Highness" only once. On a state visit to a foreign country, when a group of nobles began approaching Juliana on their knees, she turned to her Foreign Minister and said, "Mr. Luns, please have this stopped at once!"

But pomp and pageantry alone would not assure loyalty to a position most of the world considers outdated, nor is it sufficient to assert that the affection of the Dutch people for Juliana is repayment for earlier services performed by the House of Orange. Ostentatious displays by unpopular people can trigger a certain revulsion, and "What have you done for me lately?" is a universal attitude. The high regard with which Juliana is held in the Netherlands can be understood only by examining the nation's most fundamental institutions. The schools are one of the most important.

Teachers in Dutch schools extol the virtues of Juliana and constantly help engender loyalty to her with the support of parents and authorities. During Wilhelmina's reign, schoolchildren were taught to call her "Our Sunshine." Just as in American schools, where youngsters are taught patriotism by pledging allegiance to the flag, Dutch children are encouraged from the outset, with slogans such as "Long live our Queen" and "God save our Queen," to think of Juliana as a source of unity and national strength, which she may indeed be. Books praising the House of Orange are required reading: Juliana and William the Silent—Father of the Fatherland—seem, and actually are, cut from the same cloth. Also there are the holidays, loved by schoolchildren everywhere. Often these are proclaimed by Juliana, or set aside in her honor. The entire school experience promotes a warm feeling about the monarch.

Churches in the Netherlands are also supportive of Juliana and the monarchy, but in a more subtle manner than the schools. "It seems quite possible," wrote Percy Black, "that the propagation of belief through various ancient scriptures, with their copious mention of kings and queens, creates in the mind's eye of believers an orientation to society generally, and the social order specifically, that prepares them to accept and revere a not-too-dissimilar medievalism in modern garb. Moreover, the multiplicity of references to 'The King' in the doctrines of many churches may serve to elevate the concept on paper to a living thought that inveigles the mind into the more ready acceptance of 'the king' in real life."

Of course, Juliana is often seen with important church figures, which lends a certain authority to each. In addition, prayers are said in church for Juliana and the royal family, asking God to guard their health, and numerous sermons are delivered praising them. Most women who are pregnant do not have entire congregations praying for the safe arrival of their child, but Juliana did, and most of the nation would not pray for the recovery of a man injured in an auto crash, but that happened when Bernhard broke his neck in 1937. Juliana strengthens churches with her own powerful religious beliefs—her speeches are usually heavily, and sincerely, laced with references to the Almighty—and the churches in turn strengthen her and the monarchy.

Probably the most important single provider of Juliana's popularity is the press in the Netherlands, which with few exceptions is bland, conservative, and extremely solicitous in its devotion to the Queen. When the faith healer incident became public knowledge, criticism was leveled at the foreign press for "interference in Dutch affairs," rather than at Juliana for evoking memories of Russia's Alexandra. Even the Adamski episode was quickly forgotten, and many Dutch citizens, adults at the time, do not remember it took place. Perhaps typical of this type of journalism is the magazine *Holland Herald,* which in a single issue ran a headline, "Prince shoots the Queen!" (Claus took a photograph of Juliana); wrote about a lottery in which "the Queen herself is the prize" (Juliana would visit whatever Dutch town's name was drawn in a contest); reported that the Foreign Minister thought Juliana had "a great sense of humour"; quoted Bernhard that his wife had a "touching innocence"; revealed that Juliana "devotes much time to the problems of developing nations, the refugee problem and child welfare throughout the world"; pointed out that Juliana's "manner is down-to-earth"; announced that a

friend of Juliana's believed she was "natural, never demanding . . . always thinking of how other people felt
. . . too kind, in fact"; explained that Bernhard's "great
interest in cultural affairs is evident"; quoted a former
teacher of Beatrix's who called the Crown Princess "spir-
ited and charming"; and praised Claus because "he
seemed always willing to attend charity functions."

All of this may be true, but it is seldom mitigated by
the other side. Thus, when *The New York Times* called
what happened at the Beatrix-Claus wedding a "near
insurrection," a Dutch writer reported that "certain people were unhappy because Claus was German": not a
mention of the Hitler Youth. Another writer in the
Netherlands declared that the controversy over Carlos
Hugo was caused by his religion—Catholicism is the
largest religion in Holland—without talking about the issue
of Franco and fascism. Since the Dutch people are right
there and know what is happening, much of this reporting seems intended for foreign consumption. Moreover,
Juliana has on several occasions complained of the one-
sided—in her behalf!—nature of Dutch reporting, an indication that she would be willing to accept a more
realistic appraisal of her reign.

The Dutch press also attributes qualities and emotions
to Juliana and the royal family that ordinary mortals
seldom experience. For example, when Bernhard, quite
straightforwardly, agreed that Beatrix could keep a pet
dog, the writer said he "grandly acquiesced." A reader of
certain newspapers in the Netherlands might believe that
Juliana does not walk, she strides, and the reader would
learn that Juliana has "a warm and vibrant voice" that
"impresses everyone with its sincerity." Juliana "sits re-
gally," "waves expansively," and "smiles radiantly," at
the same time exhibiting "cool intelligence" and "a frugal
Dutch housewife's sound sense." It is true that the press

in the Netherlands has improved compared to earlier coverage of the monarchy, but Juliana still can be "totally absorbed" even when she is "exchanging meaningful, affectionate" glances with Bernhard, and she "obliges" rather than agrees, is "passionately concerned" instead of caring, and "vigorously expounds" rather than argues. As mentioned, there is little evidence that Juliana insists on this type of reporting, and even Bernhard, surely no opponent of the perquisites of royalty, has complained about "the highfaluting words some of the press are inclined to use about us, which mean nothing except that they imply we are not ordinary human beings."

Despite Juliana's huge fortune, apparent even to the most casual observer—$950 million said *Newsweek,* $1 billion claimed *Time* (and this before it was at least doubled by inflation)—Dutch publications appear to feel obligated to prove she is struggling along. One Dutch magazine wrote that "the House of Orange might be placed high on the world's list of richest families, but the crown jewels of the Netherlands are of surprisingly little value. In fact, the crown itself is gold plate and worth only an estimated $1,700."

This piece of writing, if not intentionally deceptive, certainly could have led to confusion. Much later in the article the reader learns that while the royal crown itself may be worth $1,700, what is *attached* to it is worth a fortune: "this consists of a narrow gold band containing four large, oval-shaped rubies, four oblong sapphires and eight smaller round emeralds" plus eight gold leaves and sixty-four pearls.

Although Juliana is already enormously popular, it is evident that much of the press believes she must be constantly praised, the public must continuously be reminded of her worth, and her fortune must be downgraded. This strategy has probably helped to maintain her popularity at consistently high levels, even though her own performance in office has undeniably helped, but it has subjected the Netherlands to criticism from abroad for its worshipful treatment of the monarchy. The following, written shortly after Juliana became Queen, is illustrative: "The Netherlands will regain its former prosperity and glory under the reign of the new Queen. This conviction is rooted in the soul of the nation. The people have faith that their future is safely entrusted to Queen Juliana. Because they know that the daughter has been a willing and eager pupil of the mother. And they also know that Queen Wilhelmina, through her life and her life work, has prepared a fertile soil that will bring forth its fruits in the years to come."

But there is more to Juliana's popularity than that engendered by schools, churches, and the press. To many Dutch people she symbolizes national unity, "stands above parties," unifies a nation split into many rival political groups. There is fear in the Netherlands that the many rival political parties would be unable to resolve their differences without resort to violence were there no monarch to mediate disputes. It does not matter whether this is true or not: the people believe it is true.

Juliana, despite all the ups and downs of her reign, has helped herself stay in office by understanding what her subjects wanted from monarchy: they wanted the Queen to be like them, to share the same views, tastes, and prejudices. It could then perhaps be said that by glorifying Juliana they were glorifying themselves. To Juliana's credit it could be said that she often represented the very best in the Dutch people: generosity, compassion, hard work, devotion to country, love of family.

Juliana also had what is called in the United States good public relations. On numerous occasions she was in the news being photographed opening a new hospital, dedicating a new school, or lending her name to some worthwhile charitable relief agency. She presented awards to deserving artists and writers, who vied with one another for the honors. The winners were forever in her debt; the losers could always look ahead to next year. Juliana attended plays and musical events, and her presence could assure a big hit; no one who was ignored by the royal family wanted to complain for fear that a later potential success might fail because of the lack of attendance by a member of the House of Orange. In this manner was support at least in part assured from the nation's intellectuals.

All of Juliana's projects and appearances appeared *good* in the eyes of the people—who could object to hosting a dinner for distinguished scientists?—as opposed, say, to a politician's wanting to raise taxes (the Netherlands has one of the highest tax rates in the world on income, one of the lowest for capital gains), and Juliana, to many people in Holland, became indistinguishable from that which was considered desirable. Working people and the poor wanted disability checks delivered on time. So did Juliana. Small manufacturers and shop owners wanted a market for their wares—flags, programs, commemorative commodities—and few items sold faster than those with a tie-in to the royal family, just as the hotel business was never quite so good as when a monarchical spectacular was taking place: Amsterdam became the fourth most popular tourist city in Europe, right behind Paris, London, and Rome. Even important industrialists hoped Juliana prospered, for she was one of them. In short, there were objective reasons for all of Dutch society to support the Queen.

What is called the "Secret of Soestdijk" also adds to the mystique of Juliana's House of Orange. Ministers frequently consult with her at Soestdijk Palace, but none has ever been forthcoming about what was discussed. "These talks," said the respected Dr. Joseph Luns, Foreign Minister for more than half of Juliana's reign, "were among my most rewarding and interesting aspects of being Foreign Minister. The Queen was always well-informed, knew the details, and often had original and fresh reaction and remarks." What these "original and fresh" remarks were remain part of the Secret of Soestdijk, but Dutch critics of the monarchy maintain that the secret is kept because what the gentle Juliana offers is naive and heavily laden with religious mysticism.

However, simply to visit the Netherlands is to understand a portion of Juliana's popularity, and that of the House of Orange. Juliana's face kindly smiles out from postage stamps, as does Bernhard's; houses and streets are named for her and her renowned ancestors; statues proclaim the greatness of the House of Orange; laws bear her signature and authority. Juliana seems part of the very air the Dutch breathe, and few question whether monarchy, *hereditary* monarchy at that, is the ideal form of government.

The family unit is yet another tremendous source of support for Juliana. Religious leaders and journalists alike laud her exemplary behavior as wife and loving mother. It would not be enough if they were simply deceiving the public: no one in the Netherlands any longer believes that Bernhard is a devoted family man. But people in Holland sympathize and identify with their very human Queen when rumors fly about Bernhard's latest alleged romance, or the willful Beatrix's marriage to her German husband. People in the Netherlands suffer right along with their Queen, cursing her enemies and praising her friends. Families hang up pictures in Juliana's honor, stories are read to children of the exploits of William the

Silent, and always the children are reminded that Juliana comes from the same stock as the great liberation leader. And of course there are always the celebrations that accompany a royal birth, so frequent when Juliana's children married, with many families feeling as if they had adopted the new Prince or Princess as their own.

"I do not think," Wilhelmina once said, "that any country will take the last steps to communism when its citizens can walk past the palace windows opening straight into the street and see their Queen knitting in the windows." Wilhelmina did indeed knit in the windows, and Juliana too embodied the stolid virtues of the Dutch. The fact that she was very rich hardly damaged her reputation in a nation that, like the United States, views great wealth as a symbol of virtue.

But there is something else that influences the people of the Netherlands to retain Juliana. Percy Black called it "Reciprocal Complementarity," a "vicarious gratification of the people's desire to be responsible for an all-important entity." A monarch could not exist without subjects, and the subjects know it. They often take a vicarious joy in seeing one among them living as they all wished they could. Everyone, of course, cannot live this way, but it is enough that they can provide for one. The higher Juliana lives, the more grandiose her style, the more elaborate her residences, even as her wealth is played down to show solidarity with her providers, the more the populace wants to reward her. She is Holland's favorite child, and the nation, like loving parents, showers her with presents. Many in the Netherlands still call her "our Julie."

Juliana and the House of Orange receive more support from older citizens than from younger ones. Older people have grown used to her since their childhood and generally prefer what is expected rather than surprise. They know what they can expect from the plain, sincere Juliana, and the House of Orange itself represents a continuity with which they feel comfortable and safe.

Many Dutch citizens believe Juliana's greatest practical value is in her ability to get things done, to untangle bureaucratic red tape, and indeed it would be an unwise official who ignored what she suggested. Also, monarchs like Juliana and Wilhelmina, who have had long reigns, assume a great deal more power than what is legally accorded them by the Constitution. "It is impossible," wrote Sir William Anson, "to be constantly consulted and concerned for years together in matters of great moment without acquiring experience, if not wisdom. Ministers come and go, and the policy of one group of Ministers may not be the policy of the next, but all Ministers in turn must explain their policy to the Executive Sovereign, must effect it through his instrumentality, must leave upon his mind such a recollection of its methods and its results as may be used to form and influence the action of their successors."

Juliana's popularity has remained high, yet she knows her subjects can be fickle. They felt betrayed by the marriages of Irene and Beatrix, disturbed by the possibility of Beatrix's succeeding Juliana, and alarmed by events in the fiery late 1960s, events that seemed out of even the House of Orange's control. One more big shock could conceivably bring the monarchy down, and the biggest of all was yet to come. But first came a smaller tremor.

15

He's here! It's a son!

At first Juliana had reason to believe Margriet's upcoming marriage to Peter van Vollenhoven, twenty-seven, a Dutch commoner, would be a placid, pleasant affair. There seemed no cause for the outrage that had accompanied the previous two weddings, and it was reasonable to expect the people of the Netherlands would applaud such a democratic choice as the commoner van Vollenhoven. In reality, he was an unprecedented choice: no Princess of Orange-Nassau had ever married any person of Dutch nationality.

These were precisely the reasons that caused the first controversy about Margriet's marriage. Whereas the marriages of Irene and Beatrix to Carlos Hugo and Claus von Amsberg had largely been opposed by the lower and middle classes, it was the old nobility that complained bitterly about Margriet's choice of Peter van Vollenhoven, a commoner *and* a Dutch citizen. In the perspective of many nobles such a union whittled away at tradition. Change was occurring, and they had witnessed enough change in their lifetimes. The nobles were friends of

Juliana, and their criticism hurt, but her instincts told her the marriage was right. Beatrix sided with the nobility. She said she thought Margriet should marry from "our own crowd."

No problem existed, however, persuading the States-General to grant its approval and thus retain for twenty-three-year-old Margriet her rights of succession. A legislature elected by the broad mass of voters could scarcely refuse van Vollenhoven because he was a Dutch commoner. Margriet remained second in line for the throne behind Beatrix.

The engaged couple had first met in 1963 at the University of Leyden, where both were studying law. Margriet was the least well known of Juliana's daughters, having avoided the spotlight Beatrix and Irene seemed to enjoy; Juliana's youngest, Marijke, commanded more attention because of her unfortunate eye ailment. Of all the Princesses, Margriet seemed most comfortable among people outside the royal circle. She worked for a time as a nursing auxiliary on a hospital ship and grew up liking the pomp and display of monarchy even less than Juliana. This was remarkable in itself, because her life had been spent receiving flattery and praise. At *age two,* one writer said of Margriet, "her hair was somewhat darker in coloring than her sisters', with an almost olive complexion and extraordinarily penetrating blue eyes which slanted downward at the ends. This gave her a rather haughty air of peering down her nose. Her straight, aristocratic, Hellenic profile . . ."

Once Margriet gave a press interview. The questions flew fast and furious for several minutes. Then Margriet simply sat down and quit. "This is driving me mad," she said.

The day of the wedding, January 10, 1967, dawned very cold, and the streets of The Hague were packed with snow and slush. The city's police chief, Gaultherie van Weezel, had mobilized twenty-five hundred officers, but he expected no trouble. Even though the disenchanted nobles were an unlikely source of public disturbance, it was better to be prepared than risk what had happened at Beatrix's wedding in Amsterdam.

Juliana was pleased that some thirty-one of Europe's highest-ranking nobility, including Sweden's Princess Christina and Crown Princess Margrethe of Denmark, were present for the marriage. Royalty had completely stayed away from Irene's wedding; Beatrix's also had been largely boycotted; and the lack of attendance detracted from the image of the powerful House of Orange. Who attends a royal wedding is often a guide to the importance of those being married.

Royalty, including Irene and Carlos Hugo, who had come from Madrid, was most definitely on hand as the coach-led procession began, but missing were large crowds on the streets. Where were the more than a million cheering people who had poured out affection for Juliana and Bernhard? Many schools and offices had been closed in the hope of attracting large numbers. "They must have stayed home to watch on television," a policeman explained.

A smoke bomb exploded under one of the horses. Then another went off. And another. Juliana felt she was living through a nightmare, and this time she did not even know what had gone wrong. Certainly no one could object to the apolitical van Vollenhoven, a commoner.

Van Weezel's police swung into action, but it was six long hours before complete order was restored and the last arrest made. What Juliana hoped would be reported as a beautiful, tranquil, elegant ceremony instead was headlined in many nations as a scene of discord and violence. Photographs revealed smoke rising from the procession, police chasing demonstrators. It was the last thing the oft-buffeted Juliana wanted, even though the protests at Margriet's wedding were nothing compared to the near state of siege that existed when Beatrix and Claus married. The point was clear: while most people in the Netherlands were in favor of Margriet's marrying Peter van Vollenhoven, the commoner and Dutchman, they did not care enough to come out and demonstrate their support, and that left the field open for young activists.

One of the reasons for the disturbances was a strong anti-monarchical sentiment felt by a vocal minority of young people in the Netherlands. It was an opportunity to gain publicity for the distrust they held for the House of Orange and to carry on a tradition of protest at royal functions they believed had begun at the Beatrix-Claus wedding. Other protesters suspected Royal Dutch Shell was profiting from the Vietnam war, and at least one carried a sign calling for "Peace in Vietnam." Still others were angered by the presence of Irene and Carlos Hugo at the wedding, having believed that royal couple intended to stay out of the Netherlands. Perhaps the most important motivation, however, was a feeling of betrayal, a belief that the royal family, and the majority of the Dutch press, had perpetrated a misleading notion on the rest of the world by portraying Peter van Vollenhoven as a commoner and, by implication, the House of Orange as democratic because it had allowed one of its members to marry a "common" man. While it was true that the press had depicted van Vollenhoven's background, the main theme had been his commoner status, and the demonstrators wanted to expose this "fraud."

Peter van Vollenhoven really was a commoner, and Juliana certainly thought of him that way (as did most nobles), but he came from an old-line patrician family of

considerable wealth, and his ancestors included burgomasters, knights, and a director of the Central Bank. His
father was chairman of the board of prosperous Bingham
and Co., Ltd., Rotterdam. To the young protesting in the
streets, van Vollenhoven did not seem to be a commoner.

Margriet's marriage revived the old contentions between
conservatives and liberals about Juliana's raising of the
Princesses, and Juliana herself was left to worry alone.
The conservatives believed Juliana's "liberal" methods of
raising the children had led to disaster, i.e., marriage to a
commoner; and liberals said her "conservative" style had
not permitted the daughters to go far enough. In truth,
Juliana had done her best, had done what she believed
was in the best interests of her children and the House of
Orange, and had she gone further in either direction there
would have been a massive outcry from the other side.

Following the Margriet–van Vollenhoven marriage,
Juliana knew the House of Orange needed something
positive to happen. She herself was still popular, perhaps
more so because she appeared to many people to be a
decent woman victimized by events, but there seemed to
be a tide running against the monarchy. The positive
event occurred on April 27, 1967, three and a half months
after bombs had once again been thrown at a royal wedding procession. Crown Princess Beatrix, long overdue
and delivering by surgery, gave birth to an eight-pound,
six-ounce, baby *boy*. Juliana was at Beatrix's side when
the baby was born at University Hospital in Utrecht.

Guns boomed in the Netherlands for the first time since
1947—on the day Marijke was born—but before anyone
wondered whether they would stop at 51, the news was
out: a boy! The first boy in *116* years. Dutch citizens
cheered themselves hoarse each time the guns roared, all
the way to 101.

The country went crazy. Carillons rang; church bells tolled; sensible, staid Dutch couples sang patriotic songs in the streets. The bars stayed open long past 1 A.M. closing as the normally conscientious police joined the revelry for one, two, many drinks, toasting the future King with a liqueur called *oranje bitter*. Ten thousand people signed a register at Soestdijk Palace, as a present arrived every minute at Drakensteyn Castle where Beatrix and Claus lived. News of the heir's birth sped overseas. The Amsterdam Concertgebouw, entertaining at Carnegie Hall, stopped its performance to thunder out the stirring strains of the "Wilhelmus."

The baby was named Willem-Alexander Claus George Ferdinand, and he became by law next in line for the throne after Beatrix, pushing Margriet back to third, technically, but for all reasonable intents and purposes pushing her completely out of the picture. Insurance company probability tables, if they ignored that monarchy may soon not exist at all in the Netherlands, would make Willem-Alexander an overwhelming favorite to be the first King of Holland since the nineteenth century.

Willem-Alexander was named after one of the sons of William III, Wilhelmina's father, who did not live long enough to succeed to the throne.

Bernhard had been hosting a party for the King and Queen of Nepal when he heard he was a grandfather. "He's here!" Bernhard shouted happily. "It's a son!" Bernhard soon was rushing to the royal palace in Amsterdam, where he was joined on a balcony by Juliana, who had hurried from Utrecht. For the first time in far too long, they stood together above a large, wildly enthusiastic throng that loved them and the monarchy.

An important Dutch politician had predicted before the Claus-Beatrix marriage that the House of Orange would reign for only ten more years. He said, after the rioting on the wedding day, "Now it looks more like five." But *Life* magazine, seeing the celebrations when Willem-Alexander was born, wrote, "Now it looks more like another 400."

The birth of Willem-Alexander was not the only good news contributing to Juliana's popularity. Although she really had very little to do with the economy, people tended to give her credit when it went well—and to blame others when it didn't—and it was going very well indeed in the Netherlands. Between 1965 and 1968 industrial production was operating at the highest level in the European Economic Community. Inflation was a high 7 percent—fourth-greatest among industrial countries behind Japan, Denmark, and France—but wages were rising between 10 and 11 percent annually. West Germany had become the nation's largest trading partner.

One startling measure of the economic prosperity of the Netherlands was that it was one of the few countries on earth that had more invested in the United States than America had in it. In 1967 the U.S. investment in Holland was $917 million, while the Dutch had $1.4 billion invested in America. Altogether, the Netherlands had $2.25 billion invested abroad in 1967, but the remarkable comparison was the one to the United States. In a later year—1972—the total foreign investments of the United States, according to the United Nations Department of Economics and Social Affairs, was $94 billion, while foreign investments in America were only $14.4 billion. The United States had 52 percent of the world's total foreign investment, yet it owned less of tiny Holland than that bustling nation owned of it. Of course, there was more to own in the United States than in the Netherlands, but that was true for many other countries that could not approach Holland's success.

Juliana visited Canada in 1967 and Ethiopia in 1969. In

Canada she saw old friends and relatives, but in Ethiopia she witnessed what monarchy had been like in the Middle Ages. Emperor Haile Selassie, variously known as the "Lion of Judah," the "King of Kings," and the "Elect of God," was an absolute monarch, completely corrupt, and one of the richest men in the world. But his country was one of the poorest, and in its capital city, Addis Ababa, were fifty thousand prostitutes. Juliana was accorded royal treatment in Ethiopia, but she left believing more firmly than ever that her own brand of monarchy was likely to last the longer. She was right: in the summer of 1974, the King of Kings was dragged out of the Jubilee Palace and thrown into a police car. The military had taken over.

There really was not much of a comparison between Juliana's Holland and Haile Selassie's Ethiopia. The one was a modern, dynamic industrial democracy, the other was a dying feudal kingdom. The Netherlands could provide a relatively comfortable living for its citizens; the people of Ethiopia, forced for religious reasons to fast 180 days a year, were starving.

Juliana understood that as long as the economy was healthy, the House of Orange was likely to retain the throne of the Netherlands. Some observers believed Orange might keep power even if there was a disastrous depression: the reasoning was that Juliana, or her successor, might side with the people against the corporations. Certainly Juliana had performed strange and unpredictable actions during her reign, but in a real sense she was in business herself, so no one could actually be sure in which direction she might move if the situation required. In any case, that sort of economic catastrophe was not looming in the near future.

A number of foreign writers have commented that Juliana and the House of Orange are more "tolerated than loved," but such is not the impression an individual gathers upon visiting the country. Instead people talk about being willing to give her even more, about being willing to die for her. The words come out simply and sound old-fashioned, but they seem undeniably true. There is, however, definite doubt whether Juliana's popularity can be transferred to Beatrix.

A phenomenon occurred in Amsterdam in the late 1960s that seemed entirely out of character for conservative Holland. Suddenly Amsterdam became known as "The Hippie Capital of the World" as thousands of young people, many from other countries, flocked to the city to make it their home. They held love-ins at Vondel Park, smoked marijuana while lazing in the sunshine outside Dam Palace, and even became involved in the political process. At times there was trouble—the police would occasionally scatter them, and Dutch marines once went after them with clubs—and when these occurred, the majority of people in the Netherlands seemed happy. The hippies were definitely anti-monarchy, but they did not seem to be able to anger Juliana. When asked what she thought of them, she replied that she agreed with many of their ideas.

The hippies even ran for office, which prompted the London Times to run a tongue-in-cheek editorial: "Is this Holland? It is odd, to say the least, that at the municipal elections in June five seats on the Amsterdam city council and eleven percent of the total vote should have been won by gentle nihilists who are opposed to authority, motor cars and war, and in favor of wholemeal bread and helping old people." Odd it might be, but it was true, and the hippies became a source of aggravation to conservatives, particularly the old nobility. Juliana could not bring herself to denounce them.

The hippies, known as Provos, took part in a number

of actions, including joining artists who held sit-ins at the Rijksmuseum in front of Rembrandt's immortal *Night Watch*. On another occasion they joined angry workers who believed that a protesting bricklayer, Jan Weggelaar, had been murdered by the police (the official version was that he had had a heart attack). The workers and hippies became enraged with Holland's largest newspaper, *De Telegraaf,* when it said no murder had been committed and decided to storm the newspaper's headquarters. The staff of *De Telegraaf* heard that the workers and hippies were on the way and barricaded themselves in their building.

The protesters had little difficulty getting through the barricades and there was fistfighting inside. The newspaper people fought back with chair legs and fire extinguishers, and finally one of them got through to Dr. Samkalden, the Minister of Justice in The Hague.

"Samkalden here."

"Your Excellency, do you know that we are being besieged?"

"Yes, yes, Mijnheer van Loon, I've heard about it."

"Do you also know, Your Excellency, that we have been besieged for half an hour and threatened and there's no sign of police, although we have constantly asked for help?"

What had happened was that the man at police headquarters had been unable to reach Amsterdam's chief of police, who had given orders that the Dutch version of a riot squad not be used without his OK. Meanwhile, he was in conference with the burgomaster.

"It wasn't a system," one writer observed, "designed for quick decisions, even if it has a certain charm."

When the police finally did arrive at *De Telegraaf,* the workers and hippies had moved elsewhere.

Later in the day there was more rioting, something Juliana was not in favor of, but nevertheless there were points upon which she and the hippies agreed. One of these was the Vietnam war. Juliana knew what war could do to the Netherlands, and she believed the United States was damaging East-West detente with its policy in Vietnam.

The Netherlands really was a country with an unwieldy number of political parties, and it was entirely possible that Juliana did serve a unifying function, especially in view of the 1967 parliamentary election results, which were fairly typical:

	1967 SEATS
Catholic Peoples'	39
Labor Party	34
People's Party for Freedom and Democracy	17
Anti-Revolutionary Party	15
Christian Historical Union	12
Democratic	7
Communist Party	5
Pacifist-Socialist Party	4
Radical Party	3
Democratic Socialists	3
Calvinist Political Party	3
Calvinist Political Union	1
Others	7

Clearly there were numerous feuding political parties in the Netherlands, but there was one area—the military—where there was plenty of centralization. Bernhard held the following positions: Inspector-General of the Army, Air Force, and Navy; Chairman of the Joint Chiefs of

Staff; Member of the Council for Military Affairs of the Realm; Member of the Defense Council; Member of the Air Force Council; Member of the Council of the Admiralty; and Member of the Army Council. The late South African General Smuts said of Bernhard, "If the constitutional conceptions of the Netherlands would have permitted the Prince to participate actively in affairs of the State, he could have become one of the big bosses in European politics." Perhaps so, but his military duties, coupled with his interest in finance, kept him quite busy.

During Juliana's annual address at the opening of the States-General in September 1970, she announced that the Netherlands could expect a deficit in the balance of payments of 700 million guilders for the year. This was really not the bad news it seemed, as the *Financial Times Supplement* had earlier pointed out: "With the biggest port in the world, a high rate of industrial expansion, a relatively modern agricultural sector, large reserves of natural gas and a modern motorway and communications network second to none, Holland's future economic prosperity appears assured."

In that event, the future of Juliana and the House of Orange also seemed assured.

Chief among the reasons for this "economic prosperity" were the three great multinational corporate giants, Royal Dutch Shell, Philips, and Unilever. These companies, especially Royal Dutch Shell, were prospering under a government that was openly pro-business and proud of it.

The corporation in which Juliana has much of her fortune invested, as Frank Huggett pointed out in *The Modern Netherlands,* did more than merely provide a great number of jobs for the Dutch people:

The companies, particularly Royal Dutch Shell, also play an important part in lessening the brain drain by providing a cadre of retired men who can later inject the benefits of their international business experience into the Dutch company. It is the ambition of many young Dutchmen to work for one of these firms, where they often acquire a social polish and an international outlook that their formal education sometimes fails to provide. Because of the opportunities for travel and career advancement offered by these companies, there is less emigration of highly skilled men than there might be otherwise; these companies offer more than adequate opportunities for the commercially ambitious to fulfil themselves. Employees of Royal Dutch Shell who work abroad are pensioned at the age of fifty-five, when they are sometimes offered important posts at home, which makes a career with the oil company doubly attractive.

In 1970 Royal Dutch Shell operated in forty-three countries and employed 155,000 people.

The second jewel in Holland's corporate Triple Crown, and another reason why Juliana has had little to fear from the economy, is Philips, which is located in Eindhoven and employs more than 40,000 people in the city, 383,900 worldwide, and operates in twenty-nine other countries. There is a great figure of Jesus Christ that stands atop Eindhoven's main church, and it is lit at night by lamps manufactured by Philips.

The company was founded in 1891 by Anton and Gerard Philips with ten employees, but today it manufactures hundreds of products and more resembles the popular conception of a Japanese corporation than one headquartered in Europe. The mostly Catholic workers in Eindhoven are urged to be loyal to the company and the country, usually in that order, and the corporation dominates most of the city's life.

The final jewel in Holland's corporate Triple Crown is Unilever, created in 1929 through the merger of the Margarine Unie and the English company, Lever Brothers. Unilever has some 327,000 employees and operates in thirty-one countries, and foreign sales account for 80 percent of its business. Like Philips, Unilever manufactures numerous products, including food and soap. As Frank Huggett explained, "Long before multinational companies became at all common, the Netherlands was participating in three of the biggest in the world. It was the smallest country in the world with such large companies."

Visitors to the Netherlands, as Juliana likes to point out, can still see windmills and wooden shoes and plenty of bicycles. In fact, the tiny, crowded country would be an environmental horror if it had the same percentage of car ownership as the United States. But no one should misunderstand: the Netherlands is a most industrial nation.

Juliana continued to be the most conscientious of rulers, never failing to fulfill responsibilities because of illness or lack of interest. In November 1970, along with eighty other heads of state, she attended the funeral of Charles de Gaulle at Notre Dame Cathedral in Paris. Other leaders in attendance included President Richard Nixon, Soviet Premier Aleksei N. Kosygin, British Prime Minister Edward Heath, and Chancellor Willy Brandt of West Germany. At one occasion at the time of the funeral Juliana was talking with an Israeli representative when she was spotted by an Arab. The Arab made a beeline for the Queen of the Netherlands to tell her what he thought of her support of Israel, but the alert Dutch Foreign Minister saw what was about to happen and intercepted him.

Bernhard's mother, Baroness Armgard, died in April 1971 after a long, painful fight against cancer. Her concerned son called in a clairvoyant to try to ease her suffering, which seemed unusual to many Dutch citizens when they remembered his unwavering opposition to Greet Hofmans.

In August 1971 Juliana paid a ten-day state visit to Indonesia, becoming the first ruling monarch of the House of Orange ever to set foot in the country. Of course, the political climate in Indonesia had changed since the days of Hatta and Sukarno. The latter had been overthrown in a bloody coup—estimates of the dead ran as high as 1 million—reportedly engineered by the CIA. The new President, Suharto, was on hand when Juliana stepped off the DC-8 KLM jetliner.

There was plenty to remind Juliana of the former Dutch colonial presence. Many Indonesians slept on pillows called "Dutch wives." Many others still called white people *tuan,* which means "lord" or "master." A white foreigner, no matter his nationality, was referred to as *Orang Belantia*, or "Dutchman."

"I consider it a privilege," said Juliana in a speech at the official banquet, "to make the acquaintance of this great and fascinating country for the first time at the highly appreciated invitation of Indonesia's President."

"Both of our nations," said President Suharto, "are entering a new era, with fervor and also with new relations. The Indonesian people are now building their future. We are thankful for the understanding of the Dutch people toward our efforts to develop ourselves in accordance with our concepts and aspirations."

A number of Indonesians, many from the upper classes, were delighted to play host to Juliana. Others, who remembered Holland's colonial role in their country, were not so pleased. To neither side, however, did Juliana seem to be some majestic monarch returned from afar to reclaim her colony, but rather a sensible woman representing her country, and the response to her was warm.

"We can't afford not to love her," remarked one Indonesian official only half jokingly. He was referring to
the fact that the Netherlands was the largest European
investor in his country, and also a major source of foreign
aid.

Juliana also paid state visits to West Germany in
October 1971, to England in April 1972, to France in June
1972, and to Yugoslavia in July 1972. She was the same
whether her host was Communist President Tito or
England's Queen Elizabeth.

Juliana finally delivered a "law-and-order" speech about
the disruptive atmosphere in Amsterdam, but what concerned her more were the plans already being prepared
for the celebration of her twenty-fifth year on the throne.
It would be a peculiarly national celebration—glamorous
royal figures from other countries would not be encouraged to attend—and perhaps for the last time she would
again experience the tremendous affection that can flow
between subjects and a beloved monarch.

16

They are terrorists, but they have a credible motivation.

THE SITE for the major celebration of Juliana's twenty-fifth anniversary on the throne was Tilburg, chosen in a highly unusual manner only the night before. In front of nationwide television and a swarm of schoolchildren, 320 balloons, each carrying the name of a Dutch city, were dropped on Juliana, and the one she grabbed bore the name of Tilburg. It was a quiet, sedate textile city of 150,000 in the southern Netherlands, but the next day it burst forth with all the excitement and gaiety of a gigantic state fair.

The balloons floated down on Juliana on September 4, 1973, and the next morning she was in Tilburg. It had been intentionally planned that the host city would have very little time to prepare. Juliana had never completely overcome her shyness and was not at her best on formal occasions. Since Tilburg had less than twenty-four hours to prepare for her arrival, it was believed the welcome would be spontaneous, the sort to which Juliana best responded. It was felt by her court and ministers, and rightly so, that the egalitarian Dutch wanted in many

respects for their Queen to be like them; and with in-
formality, the atmosphere hoped for in Tilburg, Juliana
came across as a sensible, responsible woman not much
interested in being set apart and above.

It was a good idea, but local officials almost wrecked
it. The people could respond to Juliana in a genuine
fashion, but it seemed they could not. Juliana sat on a
reviewing stand—no splendor or magnificent robes for
her—and inspected any local group that wanted to march
past: there were hundreds of them. Schoolchildren waved
and smiled, bright and happy with their little orange rib-
bons; working groups were more respectful and reserved.
What upset the local authorities were the free-lancers who
insisted on performing for the Queen. These included
an old man in a medieval getup who threw flags in the
air, and a variety of amateur talent that sang, danced,
acted, and juggled. Juliana seemed to enjoy it all im-
mensely, yet the very spontaneity she had sought was
what unnerved the city's officialdom.

The visit to Tilburg was a success for Juliana, as was
the entire twenty-fifth anniversary celebration, and it dispelled rumors that she might use the occasion to announce
plans for her abdication. Wilhelmina had abdicated after
fifty years of rule, and the grandmotherly sixty-four-year-
old Juliana could not hope to last that long. Twenty-five
years seemed a sort of milestone, which was what started
the rumors in the first place: the House of Orange had
a record of making important decisions on historic anniversaries. A newsman gathered up his courage and
broached the subject to Juliana. No, she said, she had no
plans to abdicate. She thought Beatrix should raise her
family first before taking over the responsibilities of
Queen. Knowing eyebrows were raised at this suggestion,
since none of Juliana's four daughters had even reached
their teens when *she* was inaugurated. It was known that

Juliana and Beatrix disagreed on many subjects, but this was one of the first indications that Beatrix might have a long time to wait.

Bernhard and Claus were on even poorer terms than Juliana and Beatrix. Juliana's husband, so willing to see his wife abdicate in 1956 during the Greet Hofmans affair, had done a complete turnaround. If Juliana gave up the throne, where would Bernhard be? He had to know that most of his impressive honors had been gained because of his marriage. Also, his relationship with Beatrix had cooled as she began to suspect, and then know, that there was more to her father than the carefree, happy-go-lucky exterior. And Claus, who according to many reports had imagined himself as another Bernhard, was forty-five years old, unhappily married, and wondering if he would ever reach a position of power. He wanted Bernhard's position, and Bernhard knew he wanted it.

If Juliana knew the pendulum had swung full circle, she gave no indication. Where once her fate might have hinged on the actions of Bernhard or Beatrix, theirs was now dependent on her. Juliana seemed happy simply celebrating with her subjects her twenty-fifth anniversary of rule.

The celebration began on September 4, the date Juliana became Queen after Wilhelmina's 1948 abdication. Juliana went to Amsterdam's RAI Congress Centre to watch a ninety-minute documentary—*Juliana, Queen of the Netherlands*—commissioned by the national TV foundation and shown simultaneously throughout the country. Afterward, the twenty-seven hundred guests, mostly average citizens, and the rest of the nation enjoyed a quiz program hosted by Mies Bouwman, a famous Dutch TV personality, on "Who knows most about the history of the House of Orange?" During the ninety-minute documentary Juliana was shown saying she disliked pompous occasions and criticizing the press for its worshipful attitude toward her. That same day, of course, September 4, she also grabbed the balloon that sent her to Tilburg.

On September 5 Juliana had to leave Tilburg for a 5:30 P.M. meeting at Soestdijk to receive delegates from the Antilles and Surinam who were presenting national gifts and acknowledging her as monarch of their nations. Also on September 5 and 6, on national and foreign radio stations, there was a twenty-five-hour nonstop broadcast devoted entirely to Juliana's reign. One hour was allotted for each year: from 1948 listeners could hear her thank Wilhelmina at her inauguration; from 1953 they could hear her brave words of support for the victims of the terrible flood; from 1962 came the opportunity to relive her twenty-fifth wedding anniversary; and from 1971 came remembrances of the journey to Indonesia. Carefully played down were Greet Hofmans, George Adamski, and the marriages of her first three daughters. But that really did not matter. The Dutch people did not want to be reminded of anything negative about their Queen.

All of the Netherlands took part in the celebration, and Juliana and her ministers probably had been wise in keeping it a strictly national affair and thus concentrating the festivities on herself. For such an occasion, with Juliana's popularity soaring, important foreign nobility undoubtedly would happily have made an appearance to share in her triumph, but it was recognized and understood why people in Holland did not want to see them. Too often monarchs had seemed more interested in sharing important historic anniversaries with their peers rather than their subjects, celebrating in splendid isolation, and many of these monarchs had been overthrown.

September 5 was the biggest day of celebration. It was declared a national holiday, with all schools and offices closed, and flags, music, and fairs were featured throughout the country. There was a parade, similar to America's Rose or Orange Bowl parades, featuring floats with magnificent flower displays, and variety shows, puppet shows, and automobile races. A giant fireworks display was featured on the Zuiderpark sports grounds, and The Hague Philharmonic presented three Beethoven concerts in Houtrust Hall.

Juliana was featured everywhere. An exhibition of gifts she had received in the past twenty-five years was placed on display at the Education Museum. These included precious pieces of Hague porcelain, the Orange flag that greeted King William I when he returned from England, and the golden book presented to Juliana by The Hague municipality when she first visited that city as Queen. On September 6 Juliana hosted a typical Dutch lunch for elected politicians, a *koffietafel*. That same day she drove in an open car through The Hague to receive the cheers of her subjects.

Only a month after the twenty-fifth anniversary festivities, Juliana and the Dutch government provided support for Israel in its 1973 war with Egypt, support that was endorsed by most citizens in the country. These people felt sadness that so few Jews could be saved during the German occupation. However, OPEC nations retaliated by cutting off Holland's fuel supply for nine months. There were drastic shortages which other members of the European Economic Community refused to ease. Royal Dutch Shell, of course, could have helped, but the company, headquartered in the Netherlands, did not really consider itself a citizen of any nation: rather, with subsidiaries in forty-three countries, it regarded itself as a citizen of the world.

Another problem ministers consulted with Juliana about during 1973 and 1974 was South Africa. The "blood ties" between the Netherlands and the land of apartheid had caused a continuing and considerable migration of Dutch citizens to South Africa, an arrangement most members of the States-General said they abhorred but did little to stop. Since Holland's three biggest companies were doing business in South Africa, and since the companies were able to exert an almost controlling interest over the States-General, most Dutch politicians limited themselves to rhetoric. Juliana herself, however, was disliked by whites in South Africa. Not only had she earlier held a celebrated meeting with Dr. Martin Luther King, Jr., the civil rights leader and youngest person ever to win the Nobel Peace Prize, but she donated money to the World Council of Churches to combat racism.

Nevertheless, racism was becoming a serious problem in the Netherlands, and it was one to which Juliana had to address herself if the nation was to avoid the riots that had rocked the United States. "In some ways," said one writer, "Dutch tolerance is skin-deep, but the skin powerfully shapes it. The average Dutchman does not want his daughter to go out with a Surinamer, and he believes that Moroccans are dirty, Turks dangerous, and the Indonesians slothful and noisy. Despite this, he finds himself committed to a belief in equality and fraternity among people of different beliefs and backgrounds. Although he won't invite an Indonesian home to dinner, he wouldn't invite an Englishman or a fellow Dutchman either, unless the latter happened to do exactly what he did and had the same religion and family status."

Many Dutch citizens do seem to be clannish—*quaint* is a word often used in description—but certainly they prefer the English to the Indonesians. Many Indonesians, loyal to the Netherlands during the colonial war, had come to Holland after the defeat, and they were blamed unjustly for taking jobs away from the Dutch. Many of these people were indefatigable nationalists who believed in reconquering Indonesia and regaining their previous privileged position. Instead they were confined in the Netherlands to old, discarded German barracks, were often discriminated against in employment; and when they resorted to crime—which was surprisingly seldom in light of their status—they were treated with hostility and contempt. Most disturbing was the minority of Dutch citizens who claimed they now understood South Africa's racial policies.

The growing racism in the Netherlands, spurred on by rising unemployment, was a phenomenon Juliana and her ministers could not ignore. Earlier, in 1966, South Moluccan (Indonesian) refugees had set fire to the Indonesian embassy in The Hague, but in April 1975 something much more serious was revealed: a plot to kidnap Juliana. No one familiar with the fanatical determination of the Moluccans could deny the seriousness of the threat. Twenty-five Moluccans were arrested. They had planned to hold her hostage and to kill her if their demands were not met. Anyone who doubted their seriousness, or their ability to execute such a plot, would soon have the idea dispelled.

Dutch citizens resented people of other nationalities besides the Indonesians. These were the so-called guest workers, primarily Algerians and Turks, who were brought to the Netherlands to provide cheap labor. The workers were imported by industry to maximize profits, but found themselves blamed when unemployment figures went up. Yet the Indonesians, the Algerians, and the Turks occupied a privileged position in Holland compared to another minority. George F. Sander explained in *The New York Times:*

Most unwelcome of all, however, are the approximately 150,000 proud, highly excitable Surinamese from the former Dutch dependency on the northern shoulder of South America,

just given its independence. . . . The newcomers, most of
them seeking either political or economic security, are almost
universally disliked—first, because they are brown, with some
Creoles, Javanese and Indians thrown in; and, second, because
there is so little space (or jobs) for them. A country as large
and as rich as the United States can absorb 150,000 indigent
South Vietnamese refugees without batting an eye, but in the
Netherlands, where millions of people are living shoulder to
shoulder on a soggy piece of land half the size of West
Virginia . . . a similar influx is bound to cause a problem.

Surinam had been lost as a Dutch colony in November
1975. The history of that sad nation, where previously
Juliana had reigned as monarch, provided another burning indictment of Holland's colonialism. The country had
originally come under Dutch domination in 1667 in exchange for giving the more powerful British control over
New Netherland (New York). The Netherlands imported
African slave labor to work in what was then known as
Dutch Guiana, but most of these rebelled and managed to
escape into the jungle; later, work in Surinam was performed by Dutch-indentured slaves from India and Indonesia. Today Surinam is the second-largest supplier of
bauxite, critical to the production of aluminum, and its
economy is largely controlled by the American company
Alcoa.

Juliana thus ruled over only one nation, the Netherlands
Antilles, other than Holland as the year 1975 approached
its conclusion. This tiny colony—population only 240,000—
was enormously important, however, because of Royal
Dutch Shell's huge refineries at Aruba and Curaçao.

Juliana expected trouble, probably from the Surinamese
—many of whom had become drug addicts in their attempt to escape what seemed a pervasive racism—or from
the exploited "guest workers." But when the explosion
occurred it was set off by the South Moluccans and im-

mediately dubbed by the Dutch press as "the crime of the postwar century" in the Netherlands.

In December 1975 a band of South Moluccans hijacked a train near Beilen and demanded the release of "political" prisoners—activists who wanted a return of part of Indonesia—and an airplane to fly them out of the country. The people of the Netherlands, a nation known for its extremely low crime rate, largely shrank away in revulsion from the act of the terrorists. But then the hijackers, whose friends earlier had plotted to kidnap Juliana, began to execute hostages (one of the killings was shown on national television). Dutch vigilante organizations sprang up vowing to take matters into their own hands. Prime Minister Joop den Uyl had to appear on national television to appeal for calm.

Meanwhile, a week after the train hijacking, other South Moluccans seized the Indonesian consulate in Amsterdam. Their demands were the same as those of the terrorists holding the train. Soon the self-styled flag of the South Moluccan Republic was flying from the rooftop of the Indonesian consulate. Some 150 police, 12 marksmen on nearby roofs, and a company of Dutch marines surrounded the building. With admirable discipline they held their fire as a blindfolded hostage, a rope around his neck and a knife at his back, was displayed by a terrorist at a third-floor window. The dramatic scene, relayed by television throughout the world, made Juliana think about what might have happened to her had the kidnap plot of the Moluccans succeeded. The other focus of attention, the hijacked train near Beilen, found the entire Dutch 43rd Armored Division encircling the terrorists. An eerie twenty-four-hour daylight, created by blinding floodlights, had descended upon the train.

Juliana and her ministers met almost hourly over the

crisis, the intensity of which had absorbed the entire nation. The ministers dared not make a decision the Queen might later criticize. Throughout the Netherlands everyone seemed to have a solution, but they realized the ultimate decision was in the hands of just a few. Juliana, via her frequent briefings, knew that negotiations with the extremists were proving fruitless, but she was reported to be heartened that at least the lines of communication with them were being kept open. Juliana was a proved and determined, albeit unorthodox, pacifist, and there was no doubt that she wanted to avert bloodshed. In this conviction she was joined by a majority of ministers, although there were the inevitable few hardliners who advocated a forcible showdown.

Juliana's advice, although probably not decisive, earned for the Netherlands a worldwide reputation without equal as a country that understood how to cope with acts of terrorism. The South Moluccans who had hijacked the train surrendered after twelve days, and those in the Indonesian consulate after sixteen. Children had been held hostage on the train and in the consulate, and the government's patient and civilized handling of the crisis prevented much needless bloodshed.

"The crime of the postwar century" was soon overshadowed by a more spectacular crime, and again the perpetrators were South Moluccans. Seven of them, in late May 1977, hijacked a train in Assen and took fifty hostages. At the same time six other heavily armed South Moluccans seized a village school at Bovensmilde and took 6 teachers and 105 children hostage. Again the demands were a release of "political" prisoners and an airplane to fly them out of the country.

A climate of fear pervaded the Netherlands. Many in the South Moluccan community were afraid to leave their homes out of fear of reprisals. Dutch youth gangs were formed for the express purpose of getting revenge, although of course the majority of South Moluccans were in no way responsible for the actions of the terrorists. A government spokesman tried to ease the tensions: "They are terrorists," he said, "but they have a credible motivation."

A week went by. Two weeks. The children were released from the school, but the South Moluccans still held the teachers and many aboard the train. Relying on experience from the earlier terrorist raids, many in the nation believed the government would again find a way to avert violence. But Juliana's voice was not so strong on this occasion—the greatest scandal in the House of Orange's history had intervened—and people with more strident views were coming to the fore.

It ended on the twentieth day. Dutch marine commandos stormed both the train and the school, killing eight people, six of them hijackers. There was no sigh of relief from most Dutch citizens; rather, the general attitude was one of sadness. It seemed that peaceful Holland had taken a turn for the worse.

They were bad days for Juliana also, the most trying and heartbreaking ever, and it was unlikely she would recover as she had in the past. For in the year previous to the second terrorist raids, 1976, the most sordid scandal in Holland's history had reached straight into the royal household.

17

*Your Royal Highness, I do not even want
to talk to this crook.*

IT WAS FEBRUARY 8, 1976, when Prime Minister Joop den
Uyl, a short, nervous man, very high-strung, stood before
the States-General and told it and a shocked nation about
a possible scandal that might reach to the summit of the
Dutch government. The Prime Minister tried to be re-
assuring, but his voice trembled as he talked about what
soon would be known as "Holland's Watergate." Unlike
the real Watergate, where many were hoping Richard
Nixon would resign, few people in the Netherlands wanted
Juliana hurt.

Reports of the scandal had been circulating since December. At that time a U.S. Senate subcommittee had
heard testimony from Lockheed Vice-Chairman Carl
Kotchian that a $1 million bribe had been paid to a "high
Dutch government official." Ernest F. Hauser, a former
Lockheed employee, was more willing to talk in public:
he said the money had gone to Bernhard to assure sales to
the Netherlands of Lockheed's supersonic Starfighter.
Bernhard was Inspector General of the Dutch armed
forces and on the board of directors of both Fokker Air-

craft and KLM. Fokker had a license to assemble the Starfighters in the Netherlands. He clearly was in a key position to influence purchases.

The allegation against Bernhard came at a time when the Dutch economy was in a slump. Unemployment was running at 6 percent, double what was considered acceptable, and 250,000 Dutch citizens were out of work. But it seemed most people were on his side. They remembered his efforts during World War II, but more important was his marriage to Juliana. The Queen was so popular that even Communist members of the States-General cheered her when she delivered her annual address.

Prime Minister den Uyl announced that there would be "an inquiry into the affair" and appointed a commission to investigate. As in the earlier controversy over Greet Hofmans, members of the commission were dubbed the "three wise men" and consisted of Judge A. M. Donner of the European Community Court in Luxembourg; Henri Peschar, president of the General Chamber of Audit; and Marius W. Holtrop, former president of the Dutch Central Bank. The commission immediately was criticized because it did not have the power of subpoena, nor could it hear testimony, restrictions Prime Minister den Uyl justified by saying that to do otherwise would presume Bernhard's guilt. Dutch journalist M. S. Arnoni charged that these were restrictions not extended to any other criminal suspect.

It was revealed that in late 1959 or early 1960 Lockheed offered to give Bernhard a Jetstar to "improve the climate" for the company in the Netherlands. Instead, according to testimony taken in the United States, Bernhard was paid $1 million as follows: $300,000 in 1960, $300,000 in 1961, and $400,000 in 1962. Reportedly, Lockheed's Swiss representative, the Dutch-born Fred Meuser, hired a Zurich

lawyer, Hubert Weisbrod, to make "contacts" on Lockheed's behalf. Vice-Chairman Kotchian testified that the
$1 million was funneled to Bernhard through Weisbrod.
Actually, the money was turned over to Colonel A. E.
Pantchoulidzew, a former member of the Czarist Imperial
Guard who for many years had lived with Bernhard's
parents. Lockheed officials had paid off, believing Pantchoulidzew was a middleman between Weisbrod and
Bernhard, and one Lockheed official said he had a conversation with Bernhard in which the entire arrangement was
worked out. However, Pantchoulidzew was dead in 1976
and Bernhard was denying everything.

"If you say four words, 'It is not true,' I will print it," a
Newsweek reporter told Bernhard.

"I cannot say that," answered Bernhard. "I will not say
it; I am standing above such things."

"That, Your Highness," said the reporter, "doesn't work
anymore in the year 1976."

"I won't say that," Bernhard persisted. "I am above
such things."

Bernhard was sincere in his belief that his position was
sufficiently lofty that he should not have to answer carping
accusations. It was a stance he had assumed on other
occasions, most notably in 1971 when he suggested the
States-General be bypassed so that "government could
really get down to business without having to spend its
time answering questions."

"To the outside world," said a Dutch diplomat, "he is
a fine example of the modern Prince, but in private he be-
haves like it was still the sixteenth century."

An associate of Prime Minister den Uyl was just slightly
more kind: "He thought he was a nineteenth-century
Prince, that he could do whatever he wanted, that he was
above the law."

Stories began to be told about how Bernhard would show up at Dutch embassies around the world with printed lists of expensive food and drink he wanted for the extravagant, impromptu party he intended to throw.

Juliana was furious with Bernhard. Never in modern times had the House of Orange become so embroiled in scandal, and the fact that she suspected the trouble was coming did not ease her anger. Nevertheless, Bernhard was her husband, and she would remain loyal to him. The loyalty was not a trait Bernhard had admired when it was shown to Greet Hofmans and George Adamski, but it was something he would now have to count on to avoid imprisonment.

But the question persisted: if Bernhard was guilty, why did he do it? He had a tax-free salary of $300,000 a year, a private fortune estimated at $12 million (much of it reportedly in Exxon stock), and many people considered his wife to be the richest woman in the world. In addition, Bernhard was president of the World Wildlife Fund, a founder of the prestigious Bilderberg Conference, and he served on *three hundred* national and international boards and committees. Numbered among his friends were Giovanni Agnelli of Fiat, David Rockefeller of Chase Manhattan Bank, and Baron Edmond de Rothschild.

Juliana openly let it be known that she would consider abdication if Bernhard was not cleared. Since this was something virtually no one in the Netherlands wanted, most people in the Netherlands wished the accusations against Bernhard would stop. Juliana was fighting as best she could for her husband, but she was also conscious of the House of Orange's place in history. Prime Minister den Uyl did not want Juliana to abdicate either—it would probably bring down his government—so he resorted to praise: "Her understanding of her task," said den Uyl, "has won the Dutch monarchy a new and acceptable tenure in our modern democracy."

Carl Kotchian and Daniel Haughton of Lockheed expressed no doubt that Bernhard received the $1 million. They told the U.S. Senate committee they were "absolutely" sure of it. A Lockheed executive who sat through the executive sessions explained why Kotchian and Haughton were believed: "They simply dealt with Bernhard so repeatedly and constantly, both in business and socially, that their statements were accepted as true."

Lockheed was not the only company accused of giving bribes, but it received the most publicity, thanks in large measure to the prestige of Bernhard. In fact, some three hundred corporations would admit making improper payments. These included Gulf Oil ($4 million to South Korea's ruling political party), Northrop Corporation ($30 million in the Netherlands, West Germany, Brazil, Malaysia, Taiwan, Iran, France, and Saudi Arabia), United Brands Company ($1.25 million to Honduran officials to reduce the banana export tax), and Ashland Oil ($150,000 to the President of Gabon to retain refining and mineral rights).

One of Bernhard's most damaging accusers was Ernest Hauser, who was a lieutenant of Gunther Frank-Fahle, Lockheed's agent in West Germany after World War II. Frank-Fahle had been in the industrial-espionage network of I. G. Farben that Bernhard had worked for prior to marrying Juliana. Hauser, known as the "Diary Man," stated flatly that Bernhard had received the $1 million from Lockheed. Hauser had kept careful records in his diary, and it was from that source that Bernhard was first implicated in bribery.

The people of the Netherlands were deeply shocked by the mounting accusations, but what concerned them most was that Juliana might abdicate. None of them doubted her word, and she had threatened abdication if Bernhard was not exonerated. Behind the scenes she was making it abundantly clear to Bernhard what she thought of the humiliation he had wrought on the House of Orange, and she was spending additional time in prayer. It was clear this crisis was not simply going to slip away, that it was of a much more profound nature than any she had yet faced.

The Bilderberg Conference, scheduled for March 1976, was canceled, and it soon was obvious, as Juliana had suspected, there would be more charges against Bernhard than merely taking $1 million from Lockheed. Indeed, Bernhard's whole life seemed to be crumbling apart, and it was possible he would bring the House of Orange down with him. He and Juliana were barely on speaking terms, although she would fight to the end for him, and even Beatrix had turned away. Friends of the Crown Princess said she was not the least surprised by the Lockheed revelations.

Bernhard was accused of taking another $100,000 from Lockheed in 1968 after meeting with company representatives on a Utrecht golf course. Lockheed had issued a $100,000 check to Victor Baarn, whom the company said was Bernhard. No Victor Baarn could be located, but Soestdijk Palace was located in the town of Baarn.

Bernhard was not without friends. When he was accused of conducting extramarital affairs, and more seriously of having belonged to Hitler's SS, *Time* magazine, March 15, 1976, reported, "There is no proof for any of these charges or innuendos." *Time* should have known better, although an editor later explained that "deadline pressures" might have accounted for the error. The truth was that reports were everywhere in the European press about Bernhard's romantic adventures, and in Bernhard's own semiofficial biography, published in 1962, he himself admitted membership in the SS.

The revelations came one on top of another, each more humiliating for Juliana than the one before. It was discovered that Bernhard, in exchange for a $100 million order for Dutch railroad equipment by Argentina, had paid a bribe to Juan Perón of more than $1 million. In the same transaction Evita Perón was given expensive jewelry, and a deluxe private train was thrown in for both of them. Oddly, in the eyes of some Dutch businessmen this revelation worked as a defense for Bernhard. Said one: "There's a difference, after all, between giving bribes and taking bribes."

The Perón affair brought into question the credentials of one of the "three wise men" investigating Bernhard. Marius W. Holtrop had been president of the Dutch Central Bank, which had approved the payments.

If the phrase "conflicting emotions" ever applied to anyone, it was Juliana. It seemed she was enraged at Bernhard, but at no time did she abandon him. Thus, she advanced a new argument in his behalf: the Dutch Constitution said the monarch was "inviolable," and Juliana argued that this included the monarch's husband as well.

Reports such as appeared in *Newsweek,* April 5, 1976, while not detailing indictable offenses, further eroded whatever goodwill Bernhard could call upon: "Knowledgeable sources say the Prince would sometimes mix his old 'drinking pals' with the nabobs of European business— a blend that sometimes worked and sometimes didn't. 'On one bright morning, I found myself on his private plane en route for Paris, with the champagne already flowing freely on board,' recalls a prominent Dutch businessman. 'After we arrived, we went to a plush hotel where more cold champagne and oysters were waiting. At 11 a.m., I was seeing stars, and at 2 p.m., I passed out.' The business-man also recalls a supply of attractive women—a frequent feature of Bernhard's parties."

The "attractive women" theme was particularly humiliating for Juliana, but she would not desert Bernhard because of it. She continued to defend him even after U.S. Senate sources revealed that Bernhard had used $100,000 of the alleged bribe money from Lockheed to pay for an expensive apartment for Helene Grinda in Paris.

It seemed to Juliana that the nightmare had no end. Soon it would be revealed that Bernhard had flown freely —and illegally—aboard KLM. It was a minor charge, but it added to the cumulative effect.

The relationship of Bernhard to Swiss banker Tibor Rosenbaum came under scrutiny. Rosenbaum was a larger-than-life character who was a gunrunner for the Stern Gang in Palestine and, amazingly, became Ambassador to Austria for black Liberia. Rosenbaum had founded the International Credit Bank of Geneva in 1959 and became a close friend of Bernhard's after being introduced by Baron Edmond de Rothschild. As the *Sunday Times* of London reported, "As much as ninety percent of the Israeli Defense Ministry's external budget flowed . . . through Rosenbaum's bank on the Rue de Conseil General."

In 1967 *Life* magazine charged that the International Credit Bank had been a "laundry" for $7 billion to $8 billion of mob money skimmed from Las Vegas and Caribbean casinos. The bank was a favorite of Meyer Lansky, the organized crime figure who dominated much of American gambling.

Rosenbaum and Bernhard remained friends despite Rosenbaum's connections with organized crime. Bernhard even brought the banker to Soestdijk Palace to speak to leading Dutch bankers. "I thought," said one listener, "why is this man of that tiny bank teaching us something we know so much more about?"

The presence of Tibor Rosenbaum, and others who believed they were welcome at Soestdijk because they had donated to the World Wildlife Fund, had always been a source of discontent for Juliana. The responsibilities of a monarch, and the tradition of the House of Orange, had been ingrained in her by Wilhelmina, and they did not seem to Juliana to include hosting wheeler-dealer financiers of dubious reputation.

Bernhard continued to introduce Rosenbaum into the highest levels of international social and financial society. Then, in 1974, Bernhard sold a castle he owned, Warmelo in eastern Holland, formerly occupied by Baroness Armgard, to a firm in Liechtenstein called Evlyma, Inc., for $400,000. The purchase price was far less than the castle was reportedly worth, and there were printed suspicions in the Dutch press that Bernhard had secretly stashed away part of the money, suspicions that were strengthened when it was discovered that Evlyma, Inc., was owned by Rosenbaum's International Credit Bank.

In 1975 Rosenbaum's bank was broke and he stood accused of fraud and embezzlement by Baron Edmond de Rothschild in connection with millions of dollars de Rothschild had deposited in behalf of Israel.

The charges against Bernhard grew much more serious. The West German Christian Social Union leader, the ultrarightist Franz-Josef Strauss, charged that West German Chancellor Helmut Schmidt made an offer to Bernhard of *$40 million* if he could persuade the Netherlands to purchase Northrop's F-14 Cobras. Whether the reactionary Strauss had his own personal motives in making the accusations is still unclear. Schmidt denied the accusation, but critics of Bernhard claimed that Strauss was in a position to know: he had been West Germany's Defense Minister. On the other hand, Ernest Hauser, the "Diary Man," claimed that Lockheed had paid $12 million to the Christian Social Union to pave the way for sales of Lockheed's Starfighter.

The evidence against Bernhard in the instance of the $1 million seemed solid and compelling. But the bribe itself, Juliana knew, was not the most potentially dangerous part of the episode. The Starfighter Bernhard allegedly urged on the Dutch people was a patently unsafe airplane that had earned the nickname "the Widowmaker." As author Jim Hougan, also Washington editor of *Harper's*, pointed out, "Of 900 Starfighters sold to the Germans, 174 crashed (in peacetime), killing 96 pilots. In Japan, 60 of 230 crashed." Hougan also explained what Juliana was most worried about: "The outrage felt by the Dutch, the Germans, and the Japanese at learning of the bribes is consequently something of a family affair. Some of the widows and next of kin see a direct connection between their loved ones' deaths, the choice of an inferior plane, and the licentiousness and greed of potentates."

The one quality Juliana had most assiduously presented to the people of the Netherlands—and it was a quality she possessed—was her concern for them and their welfare. Had the shoddy construction of the Starfighters been made an issue in the Dutch press, Juliana would have been forced to reconsider her all-out support of Bernhard. Certainly she could not have ignored the story, if it had taken place in Holland, that struck the West Germans as bizarre and grisly: a West German general, reportedly the recipient of Lockheed's largesse, lost his son in the crash of a Starfighter.

Juliana found it torturous to follow her husband's twisted trail as it gradually was unraveled by the world's press. It turned out that another friend of Bernhard's had been Robert Vesco, the fugitive financier currently accused of looting Investors Overseas Services, Ltd., of $224 million, an accomplishment generally acknowledged to be the largest single swindle in the history of the world. In 1970 the thirty-four-year-old Vesco had begun to take over IOS from Bernie Cornfeld and by 1971 was already suspected by the Swiss government of looting the company. Interestingly, one of the early investors in IOS was Dewi Sukarno, the stunningly beautiful wife of the overthrown Indonesian leader, who once pulled pearls and diamonds out of her brassiere and begged an IOS executive to invest them for her. Dewi Sukarno would later become a friend of Helene Grinda's.

With Swiss authorities breathing down his neck, Vesco desperately needed a new base of operations. Soon he was writing to tell clients to send their money to Post Office Box 10331 in Amsterdam. Vesco did not bother to mention that sending these payments was illegal unless the company's name was registered with the local chamber of commerce, which Vesco's was not. Oddly, it seemed at the time, the Dutch police did not shut Vesco down.

Vesco flew to West Palm Beach, Florida, in February 1972 and met with Bernhard, who was presiding at an art auction. Vesco bid $18,000 for a painting of a leopard that experts said was worth much less and donated $10,000 to the World Wildlife Fund. Soon he was a guest at a Soestdijk Palace reception.

"Bernhard," recalled a banker who was at the reception, "tried to push this Vesco into my lap. He said, 'This is a great man; he is going to clean up IOS. You should give him an office at your bank.' I said, 'Your Royal Highness, I do not even want to talk to this crook.'" Nevertheless, Vesco's friendship with Bernhard evidently paid off, since he continued to be able to do business in Amsterdam.

Robert Vesco was precisely the sort of person Juliana did not want around Soestdijk Palace. The House of Orange did not want to be associated with the individual accused of history's largest swindle. In addition, a great deal more had come to light about Robert Vesco in 1976 than was known when he was a guest at Soestdijk. For instance, there was a mysterious $200,000 donation—for which there was no receipt—to Richard Nixon's 1972 reelection campaign. Also, Vesco had hired Donald Nixon, the former President's nephew; and Vesco himself, after establishing himself as a fugitive in Costa Rica, was widely reported to be involved in major drug-smuggling operations. There were also allegations of Vesco's connections with the CIA, and indeed, at his Costa Rican retreat many of his bodyguards were former CIA employees.

In any event, Bernhard's connection with Lockheed was what continued to fascinate investigators the most. It seemed the relationship had an exceptionally long run. The most damaging evidence of all against Bernhard stemmed from a 1974 letter he wrote to Lockheed suggesting that he be paid a "commission" on purchases by the Dutch government of Orion antisubmarine aircraft. As outlined by Bernhard, the "commission" would have amounted to between $4 million and $6 million. Lockheed officials thought the amount was too high, prompting an outraged Bernhard to write to former Lockheed Vice-President R. B. Smith:

My Dear Mr. Smith.
The message you gave my secretary by phone and your confirmation in writing was, to say the least, disappointing as you can imagine. It occurs incredible [sic] that this proposal would be rejected like this without dialogue and discussing details for other possibilities.
This would never have occurred in the days of Bob or Courtlandt Gross [former Lockheed officers].

Since 1968 I have in good faith spent a lot of time and effort to push things the right way in critical areas and times and have tried to prevent wrong decisions influenced by political considerations.

I have done this based on my old friendship with Lockheed—and based on its past actions.

So I do feel a little bitter. Any proposal can be modified—but at this point also in view of diplomatic pressure put on—by someone, you'll guess who—I feel that I will not do any more about this procurement program. What's more I will say so when consulted.

The letter made an impression when it was forwarded to Lockheed. R. B. Smith was authorized to offer Bernhard $1 million, but the money was never paid, reportedly because the sale of the Orion aircraft fell through.

Carl Kotchian of Lockheed offered one reason to the U.S. Senate why Bernhard might need money: "Bernhard would have you believe the Queen has him on a tight budget." Dutch journalists, while generally agreeing with this assessment, offered additional possible motives. One of these maintained that Bernhard had mistresses in Tanzania, the Ivory Coast, and Mexico, and he speculated that one of them could be blackmailing the Prince. Also, of course, despite whatever personal fortune he had and his $300,000 salary, Bernhard lived extravagantly, and the simple truth might have been that he needed additional income to maintain his accustomed life-style.

The "three wise men" presented their findings to Prime Minister den Uyl, and all that remained for den Uyl was to work out with Juliana the language to be used in the public report. This was extraordinary since other criminal suspects or their spouses were not consulted about how to inform the public about the charges against them, but this was not the average criminal case and its consequences could alter the course of the nation. What was even more remarkable was that den Uyl *had* to consult with Juliana before issuing the report, since he needed her permission as monarch.

Despite evidence that was called "overwhelming," Juliana stuck by her husband and insisted that the government report clear Bernhard. Her husband, variously described as "defeated" and "a shadow of his old self," thought for a moment there might actually be hope. But it was simply impossible, den Uyl argued; too many people already were aware of much that had happened. It was bound to come out. Den Uyl promised the report would be as mild as he could make it, but certain things would have to be said; Bernhard would have to resign from his posts, and at the least he would have to make some sort of admission or apology. Already on the record in the United States, den Uyl pointed out, was sworn testimony that Lockheed would "never do business again in the Netherlands" unless Bernhard was given $4 million.

Juliana played her trump card: she said she would abdicate if Bernhard's name was not cleared. Abdication would topple den Uyl himself. But the Prime Minister immediately overtrumped, and the royal couple was forced to surrender. If Juliana abdicated, den Uyl said, Bernhard would probably be prosecuted criminally. He could be sent to prison. But if Juliana remained on the throne, Bernhard was safe. It was unthinkable that the husband of the nation's ruler would be incarcerated, and jail, den Uyl reasoned, would be the ultimate disgrace for the House of Orange.

Prime Minister den Uyl had in reality plea-bargained with Juliana and Bernhard, and his performance was very adept. He kept his own government from collapsing, and if everyone was not pleased, at least they could live with the solution. Den Uyl earlier had been accused of bungling when he endorsed George McGovern over Richard Nixon in the 1972 U.S. presidential election, but even opposition politicians in the Netherlands professed admiration for his handling of the Lockheed affair.

On August 26, 1976, the Dutch commission released its report, which immediately became a best seller in the Netherlands. The report said that Bernhard had been open to "dishonorable requests and offers," that "His Royal Highness was the intended recipient of the one million dollars, which was meant for his benefit alone," that "the Prince's actions have damaged the national interest," and that "from time to time substantial sums of money would be presented to H.R.H. by companies on the occasion of the opening of factories and anniversary celebrations, etc., intended for charitable purposes, sometimes expressly specified by the donor and sometimes not."

This last reference was perhaps the most devastating in the entire report. It revealed the potential for deep-running corruption, because Bernhard had never been known to give away large sums of money. Officials at the World Wildlife Fund claimed they had never received a donation from him for more than $10,000.

"To sum up," the report read, "the commission has come to the conclusion that H.R.H. the Prince in the conviction that his position was unassailable and his judgment was not to be influenced, originally entered much too lightly into transactions which were bound to create the impression that he was susceptible to favors."

"The general reaction is shock," said H. A. M. Hoefnagels, editor-in-chief of a major Dutch newspaper. "It's far worse than what the general public thought. We don't know how to react to this. We are all just shocked."

"We had a nice country," said Piet Dankert, chairman of the parliamentary committee on military appropriations, "and the royal family was the perfect household. That myth is all blown up now." This criticism from Piet Dankert had special meaning. Earlier he had been offered a large bribe by Dassault, the French company, to use his influence to make sales of the Mirage. Dankert had reported the bribe attempt.

Bernhard resigned his business, charitable, political, and military posts on the day the report was made public. His high-flying career was probably over. So also, many people in the Netherlands suspected, was his marriage, although it probably would not end in divorce after already having survived so many stormy years.

Bernhard issued his own statement. It had been insisted upon by Prime Minister den Uyl to counter expected opposition from conservatives who might claim Bernhard was the victim of a liberal conspiracy. The statement was carefully worded and admitted the minimum:

The report from the three-man commission has convinced me that my relations with Lockheed, in my friendship of many years with several highly placed officials of the company, have developed along the wrong lines. In particular, I have not observed the caution in this matter which is required in my vulnerable position as consort of the Queen and Prince of the Netherlands. I admit and sincerely regret this.

I have not been critical enough in my judgment of initiatives presented to me. I have written letters that I should not have sent. I accept full responsibility for this and thus accept the disapproval expressed by the commission in its report.

I have taken cognizance of the view that the Government has taken with regard to my conduct. I accept the consequences and shall resign from the functions named. I hope to retain the opportunity of serving the country and in this way, as in others, to restore confidence in me.

Bernhard did receive one piece of heartening news. A vote in the States-General calling for Bernhard's prosecution was defeated 143 to 2. Two members of the Pacifist-Socialist Party, arguing for "equality before law," were the only legislators wanting him prosecuted.

Bernard Weinraub, writing in *The New York Times,* searched for reasons for Bernhard's downfall: "Many Dutch officials and journalists attribute the Prince's plunge into the murky Lockheed waters to his restlessness, his long-standing friendships in the International Jet Set, his tireless traveling with its thinly veiled implication that he considers the Dutch too plodding and earnest for his tastes."

Dutch journalist Willem Oltmans, who knows Bernhard, had a similar assessment: "Bernhard had a distorted view of the Dutch people, and of his own position. He thought he could not be touched."

If Bernhard had thought of the Dutch as "plodding" and unworthy of his attentions, he could be thankful for one such steady individual. Without Juliana, steadfast, reliable, he almost certainly would have suffered much more than just humiliation.

18

Juliana likes *to be Queen. . . . She'd be
lost if she ever abdicated, and she knows it.*

WILL JULIANA ABDICATE?" or "When will Juliana
abdicate?" are the two questions that most frequently
arise in the Netherlands when the subject of the monarchy
is brought up. "No" and "I hope not for a long time" are
the most welcome answers. But the talk about abdication
is so pervasive, almost part of the very air, that the conversation inevitably turns to *when*.

Many Dutch citizens thought Juliana would step down
from the throne after the critical commission report on
Bernhard's activities. Most were happy she did not, but
perhaps more important than the mass sentiment were the
prominent and influential individuals who believed abdication was the best solution. They were convinced it was
the least painful way of ushering the distinctly embarrassing Bernhard out of the limelight. How, these people
reasoned, could foreign nations and even the Dutch themselves have confidence in a government headed by a
Queen whose husband had been disgraced? A number
of people holding this view, however, many of them
politicians, saw nothing contradictory in November 1978,

when they applauded the announcement by the Netherlands that it would purchase thirteen Orion naval reconnaissance aircraft from Lockheed for $290 million. Evidently Lockheed could be forgiven, but not Bernhard.

The date of Juliana's expected abdication gave rise to a grim guessing game in the Netherlands. Everyone took part in the joyless parlor sport, and all had an opinion. The commission report had been issued on August 26, 1976, and some believed Juliana would abdicate as early as September 4. That was the date Wilhelmina had stepped down twenty-eight years earlier, and people knew how conscious of anniversaries the House of Orange had always been. But the day passed without Juliana's even being in the country. In a demonstration of solidarity for her beleaguered husband, she had left on a vacation with Bernhard.

The next predicted date for abdication, suggested with tongue in cheek by the irreverent, was January 7, 1977. That was her fortieth wedding anniversary, and since Bernhard was the cause of her problem it was proposed that she mark the day by relinquishing her throne.

More serious guesses centered on April 30, 1977, and May 12, 1977. April 30 would be her sixty-eighth birthday, and May 12 was the date Wilhelmina had announced she *intended* to abdicate: it would be the 128th anniversary of Juliana's grandfather William III having become King. But these dates also went by, and if Juliana had fixed a time for abdication in her mind, she was keeping it to herself.

Meanwhile, Juliana's daughters, the four Princesses, had gone their separate ways. The youngest, Princess Marijke, was married in 1975 to Jorge Guillermo, a most unusual choice. Guillermo, a Cuban refugee, was a teacher and fund-raiser in New York City for the Addie May Collins

Shelter of Harlem, a center for preschool children. He and his brother had left Cuba in 1960 with their father, a physician, and their mother, who held two doctorates from the University of Havana and had been Minister of Higher Education before Castro took over. She was currently teaching Spanish at Hood College in Frederick, Maryland. Jorge Guillermo was a graduate of Miami Senior High School and of Monmouth College in Monmouth, Illinois, with majors in history and art. According to Stafford Weeks, the dean at Monmouth, Guillermo "was a very, very bright boy. He was very well read, very articulate and very informed. He was the type of student who had varied interests and very strong opinions." Guillermo worked for two years at Chase Manhattan Bank and quit, according to a friend, because "he hated it."

Juliana announced Marijke's engagement on St. Valentine's Day, 1975, and it was accepted without complaint by the Dutch people. Marijke, twenty-seven years old and partly blind, had always been a favorite of the Dutch. Also, this was before the Lockheed revelations, with the House of Orange's popularity extremely high. Marijke, ninth in line for the throne, helped guarantee a friendly reception by saying she would not ask for approval of the marriage from the States-General, which meant that she and any of her descendants had forfeited their right to rule in the Netherlands. The "problem" was that her fiancé was Catholic, although approval almost certainly would have been granted if requested.

Marijke had studied music in Montreal and then taught at a Montessori school in New York City, where she met her future husband. They enjoyed going to the opera (he was writing a book about opera) and standing "in line like everybody else" to buy movie tickets, an experience Juliana treasured from the wartime years in Canada.

Marijke had been able to live unnoticed in Manhattan as Christina Van Oranje.

Deirdre Carmody of *The New York Times* attended the press conference at the residence—14 East Ninetieth Street—of the Dutch Consul General, where the American announcement of the engagement was made, a press conference that "began with intimidating formality. William Campagne, the Consul General, welcomed everyone and then a voice in the back of the elegant room proclaimed: 'Her Royal Highness and Mr. Guillermo.'"

Marijke was asked how she had come to know "Mr. Guillermo."

"I knew Mr. Guillermo—" she began.

"Oh, you can call me George," he interrupted.

Jorge Guillermo soon proved he could maintain his sense of humor.

"Did you expect someday that you would marry a princess?"

"No."

"Were you happy when you learned Christina was a princess?"

"Yes."

"How did you propose to her?"

"On my knees."

Marijke was asked what they had done on their first date.

"We went to a dinner party," she said in flawless English.

"What about the second date?"

"We went to a dinner party."

"We like dinner parties," explained Guillermo.

Marijke and Jorge Guillermo were married in June 1975 in Utrecht Cathedral. European royalty had not been encouraged to attend, but there were eleven hundred

guests inside the church for the ceremony that was performed by both a Catholic priest and a Protestant clergy-
man. Afterward, little Princess Marijke rode through the
streets of Utrecht being cheered by tens of thousands of
her countrymen. They had suffered with her through her
eye affliction, and to many a Dutch citizen she seemed
almost a member of the family.

Marijke and Jorge Guillermo announced they would
make their home in New York City.

Margriet and Peter van Vollenhoven continued to live
in the Netherlands, and most fear of his upper-class background was soon dissipated. He seemed to be a casual
sort of young man, more happy playing popular tunes on
a piano than exercising business or political leadership.
Margriet remained the only other one of Juliana's daughters still in the line of succession, but it would take an
inconceivable disaster to Beatrix's family before she would
be in serious consideration. Margriet and Peter van Vollenhoven have four sons.

Irene and Carlos Hugo maintain residences outside the
Netherlands, but they are often seen inside the country
also. Members of the Jet Set and often sought for parties
thrown by the Beautiful People, Irene and Carlos Hugo
have softened their politics considerably and now profess
that the ideal form of government is a democratic monarchy. Many in the Netherlands remember their earlier
stand for fascism, when it seemed Carlos Hugo might
be smiled upon by Franco, and they appear to be dubious
at best. Irene and Carlos Hugo, like Margriet and Peter
van Vollenhoven, have four children, and the children
could conceivably become important if Carlos Hugo's
claim to the Spanish throne—now occupied by Juan
Carlos, the son of Don Juan—ever becomes a serious possibility: Prince Carlos Javier Bernardo, born January 27,

1970; the twins—Prince Jaime Bernardo and Princess Marguerita Maria Beatrice—born October 13, 1972; and Princess Maria Carolina Christina, born June 23, 1974.

And finally there is Crown Princess Beatrix, who on several occasions has annoyed her mother and the people of the Netherlands by expressing impatience that she is not yet Queen. Beatrix, who turned forty on January 31, 1978, does not seem to be a particularly popular or widely loved figure in the Netherlands. Many Dutch citizens resent what appears to be eagerness on her part to replace her respected mother; and Beatrix's personal manner, often described as high-handed with "a trace of arrogance," also contrasts unfavorably with Juliana's.

Beatrix and Claus have three sons: Prince Willem-Alexander Claus George Ferdinand, born April 27, 1967; Prince Johan Friso Bernhard Christiaan David, born September 25, 1968; and Prince Constantijn Christof Frederick Aschwin, born October 11, 1969. These male heirs, it is hoped in some Dutch circles, will provide a solution for what is feared would be an extremely unpopular reign by Beatrix. If she would abdicate shortly after Willem-Alexander came of age—and most Dutch citizens do want a King—the monarchy might survive a short period of Beatrix on the throne.

In any event, Wilhelmina's House of Orange, which seemed about to vanish before Juliana was born, now has Beatrix and Margriet in the line of succession, plus seven of Juliana's grandsons. The ruling family of the Netherlands at least appears secure in this respect. The length of time it will actually survive on the throne is another matter, which was an important factor in Juliana's mind as she weighed the question of abdication. There were many other factors to consider.

One was her age. She was seventy years old on April

30, 1979, and many in the Netherlands had said all along that would be the day she would step down. A few contended it had been part of the deal worked out with Prime Minister den Uyl during the bargaining over the official report. Juliana's age was a consideration, for her job was a wearing and difficult one, but she seemed as always to be in remarkable physical health, and April 30, 1979, came and went. What concerned some people, including friends, was her mental state. Each speech she delivered appeared to contain more religious references than the previous one, and even a journalist who was friendly to the monarchy called one of them "incomprehensible."

But a second Dutch journalist, also a student of her reign, did not think she would abdicate. "Get this," he said with emphasis. "Juliana *likes* to be Queen. It's all she has. There's nothing else. At least Wilhelmina could knit, but Juliana can't even do that. She'd be lost if she ever abdicated, and she knows it."

Still another theory held that Juliana would not abdicate because of Bernhard. Adherents to this reasoning believe that what was known as the "Lockheed Scandal" was only the tip of a giant iceberg, and that Bernhard was still in great peril. His best hope, therefore, was for Juliana to remain on the throne: his enemies might be more reluctant to go after him in such a situation, and it could be argued that Juliana's immunity extended to him.

But perhaps most important on the question of abdication, the Dutch people were as always in Juliana's corner, and not merely because they had reservations about Beatrix. They sensed that in Juliana they had a remarkable monarch, one whose like they would probably never see again. Old-fashioned in both thought and deed, she had earned the respect and love of a modern, democratic nation. Beset by problems caused by her own superstition, problems that would have toppled most other rulers of an industrial state, her vulnerability instead enkindled in her subjects a feeling of protectiveness toward her. Victimized by her upbringing and her own unworldly outlook, she was not ultimately blamed by the Dutch people for the marriages of Beatrix and Irene or her unfortunate alliance with Bernhard. Juliana seemed to do everything wrong; everything, that is, except fail to win the admiration of her people.

Index

Wilhelmina and, 10, 63, 80,
81, 83, 92, 103, 106
after World War II, 102–3,
105, 106
during World War II, 87,
88, 91–92, 94, 95, 97
Bernhard, Saint, 66
Bilderberg Conference, 133–
34, 215, 217
Bingham and Co., Ltd., 189
Black, Percy, 176, 183
Blaskowitz, General, 103
Bledisloe, Lord, 88
Bocca, Geoffrey, 15
Boeke School, 106–7
Bonaparte, King Louis, 31–32,
80
Borculo, the Netherlands, 60
Bouwman, Mies, 203
Boxer, Charles R., 30
Brandt, Willy, 198
Brazil, 216
British Petroleum, 138
Budge, Don, 70
Bundy, McGeorge, 133

Calvinism, 24, 120
Campagne, William, 232
Canada, 117, 126, 191, 192
Dutch royal family seeks
refuge in, during World
War II, 88–90, 92–95,
97–98, 100–101, 105, 231
Carlos Hugo, Prince, 155–62,
164, 173, 178, 185, 187,
188, 233
Carlos Javier Bernardo, Prince,
233–34
Carmody, Deirdre, 232
Carol, King of Romania, 47, 52
Catholics, Catholicism, 44, 178

Dutch war of independence
from Spain and, 23
in England, 27, 28
Princess Irene's conversion
to, 154–55, 157, 158
Central College (Iowa), 125
Central Intelligence Agency
(CIA), 223
Charles, Prince of Sweden, 61
Charlotte, Grand Duchess of
Luxembourg, 88, 150
Charter for the Kingdom of
the Netherlands, 136–38
Chiang Kai-shek, Madam, 99
Chile, 122
Christian, King of Denmark,
47
Christina, Princess of Sweden,
187
Churchill, Winston, 48, 111
Claus, Prince of the Nether-
lands, 163–73, 177, 178,
182, 185, 188, 190, 203, 234
Colijn, Premier Hendricus, 79,
91
Collier's, 108
Columbia University, 125
Congress of Vienna, 31
Constantijn Christof Frederick
Aschwin, Prince, 234
Constantine, King of Greece,
88, 173
Cornfeld, Bernie, 222
Coty, René, 7
Cullman (Alabama) Coal and
Coke Company, 43
Current Biography, 42
Cuyp, Aelbert, 25
Czechoslovakia, 88

Dankert, Piet, 226–27
Dassault company, 227